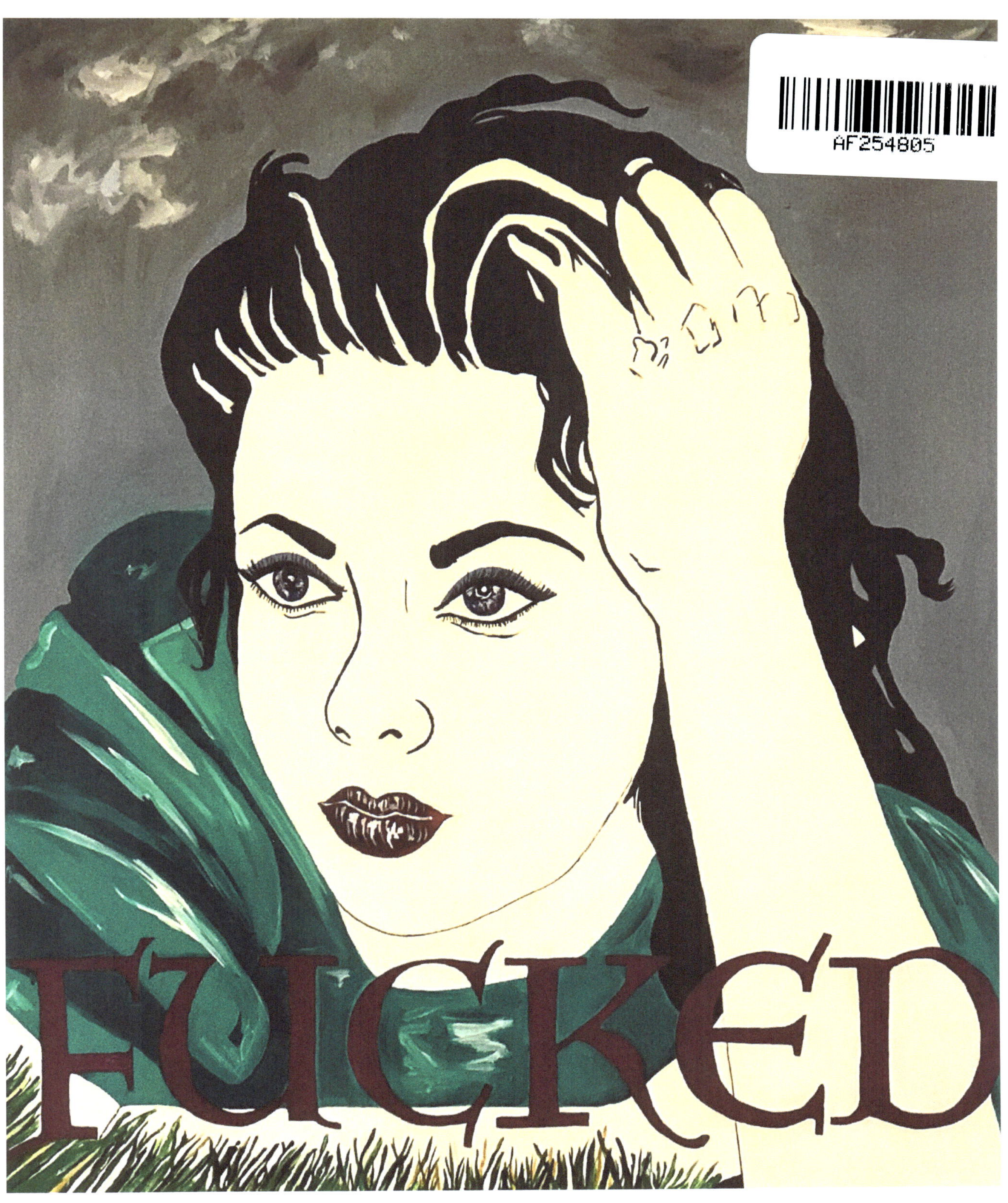

Kathe Burkhart *Fucked: from the Liz Taylor Series (publicity photo)* 2020
Acrylic and body jewelry on canvas 93 x 79 cm

Erin M. Riley

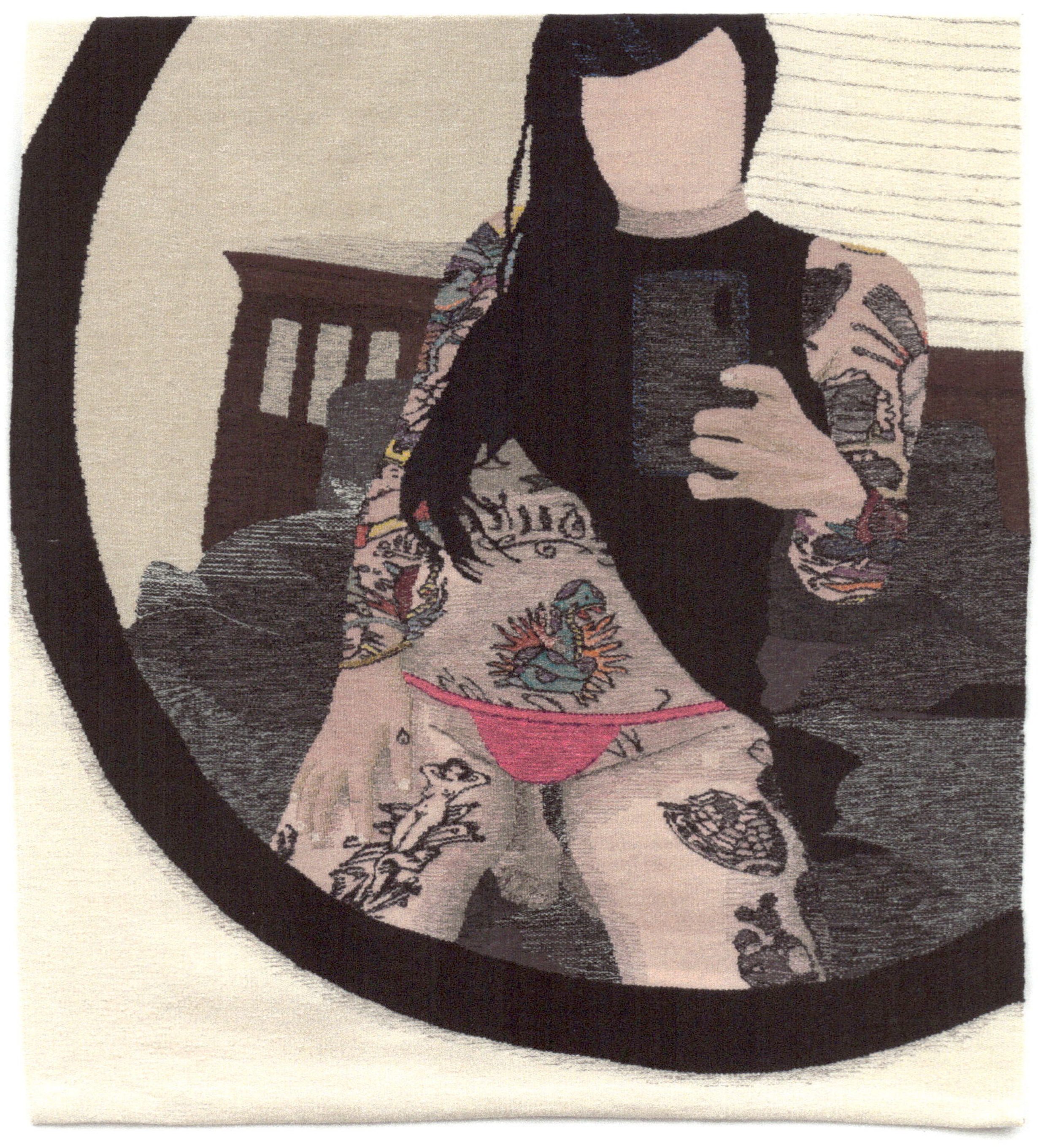

Nudes 42, 2020, wool, cotton, 54 x 48 in.
Courtesy of **Erin M. Riley** and P·P·O·W, New York

The Edgy Issue

Publisher and Editor: Jeffrey Cyphers Wright
Deputy Editor: Ilka Scobie
Associate Editor: Lori Ortiz

Cover art: JCW; Design: LO

Box 1215 Cooper Sta. NY NY 10276

https://livemag.org
SUBSCRIBE!

Penny Arcade

Ballerina

Ballerina 1

I make friends with cities the way the other people make friends with people. Perhaps it is because my need for solitude and sanctuary has always been so great.

As a child, in my immigrant, Italian mother's house, even grown up, I was never allowed to close my bedroom door, nor be alone for any period of time.

Instead, I found sanctuary where they could not follow me; the empty railroad tracks behind my house, the black acid plateau below the dump, the jagged granite outcrop, on my way to school, every day, high up, my back against the rock, the sun on my face.

Spread your wings
Come on fly awhile
Straight to my arms
Little angel child

We can find many things in other people but sanctuary and solitude are not among of them. No matter how kind, how non-judgmental, or even how silent, not even a lover can hold our solitude or offer us sanctuary. Solitude cannot be shared. It can only shelter one, and we must never turn another person into a sanctuary.

I know many people cannot fathom New York City as a place of solitude or sanctuary, but for some of us, for many of us, that cacophonous, scurrying, chaotic place held a holy peace. The asphalt jungle they called it in the 1960's, boundaried by danger and risk—physical, emotional, cultural, intellectual risk.

And we who needed that raw, unmapped landscape, craved it with a desperation as great as the bleakness that emanated from its haunted streets.

SFX 23 – X into Ballerina 3

You know you're only
Lonely twenty-two story block

That bleakness flowed and met the desolation of our own hearts, the way the sea washes back into its tributaries.

We who fit nowhere else.
We who ground to the granite ignite below our feet.
We who fled the myopic, claustrophobic, Puritanism of America's interior, breathed free though ragged in its harsh embrace.

SFX 24 – X into Ballerina 4

Crowd will catch you
Crowd will catch you
Fly it, sigh it, try it

People talk about how the world is changing.

Well, I may be wrong

But some of us understand that the world has changed forever.

But something deep in my heart tells me I'm right and I don't think so

There are no more empty places,

You know I saw the writing on the wall

no dark alleyways, no secret corners left anywhere.

Look, New York City is only a small island. It was easy to conquer. The boroughs quickly followed. Now it is like every other city in the world, it too is now mapped, delineated, bought, sold, branded.

TIME OUT New York, TIME OUT LA, Time Out London
TIME OUT Marrakesh, TIME OUT Istanbul, TIME OUT Bangkok
TIME OUT Aleppo

When I tell people what I miss about New York, they think I am talking about the 60, 70, 80's They think I'm talking about my past … a past that has been glorified to them.

They come up to me on the street, they say, Oh! Penny Arcade. I read about you in Patti Smith's book Just Kids. They associate me with that lost glory of the 70's but I stayed underground. I out-Rimbaud-ed Patti, and I equate that time as only glorious defeat.

I know from experience that my point of view is incomprehensible to some people. Why? because my point of view has been honed by a long exile at the edge of society.

SFX 25 – X into Ballerina 5 – But If It Gets To You

But if it gets to you

And sometimes it does

And you feel like you just can't go on

You can't go on talking to stupid people.

All you gotta do

Yes the world has changed.

Is ring a bell

and you…
… you need look no further than the roses.

Haven't you noticed that the roses in the shops have lost their scent? That they no longer smell like roses.
Doesn't that frighten you?
Does anyone know what I'm talking about?
Can I get a witness in this room?

William Shakespeare said, "A rose by any other name would smell as sweet," and what pray tell me is the name of the rose now …

… Incomprehensible.

The Sentinel at the Door

They were saying
we're living in the late this,
the late that.

But the this or that
was only getting started.
Sometimes it seemed

it was looking forward
(if it could look)
to going on without us.

"You can't put up with my
so-called shit?
Go live your so-called life

somewhere else.
See how you like
your new cage.

As for us, we're on our way.
The end recedes
in the rearview mirror

of our so-called car."

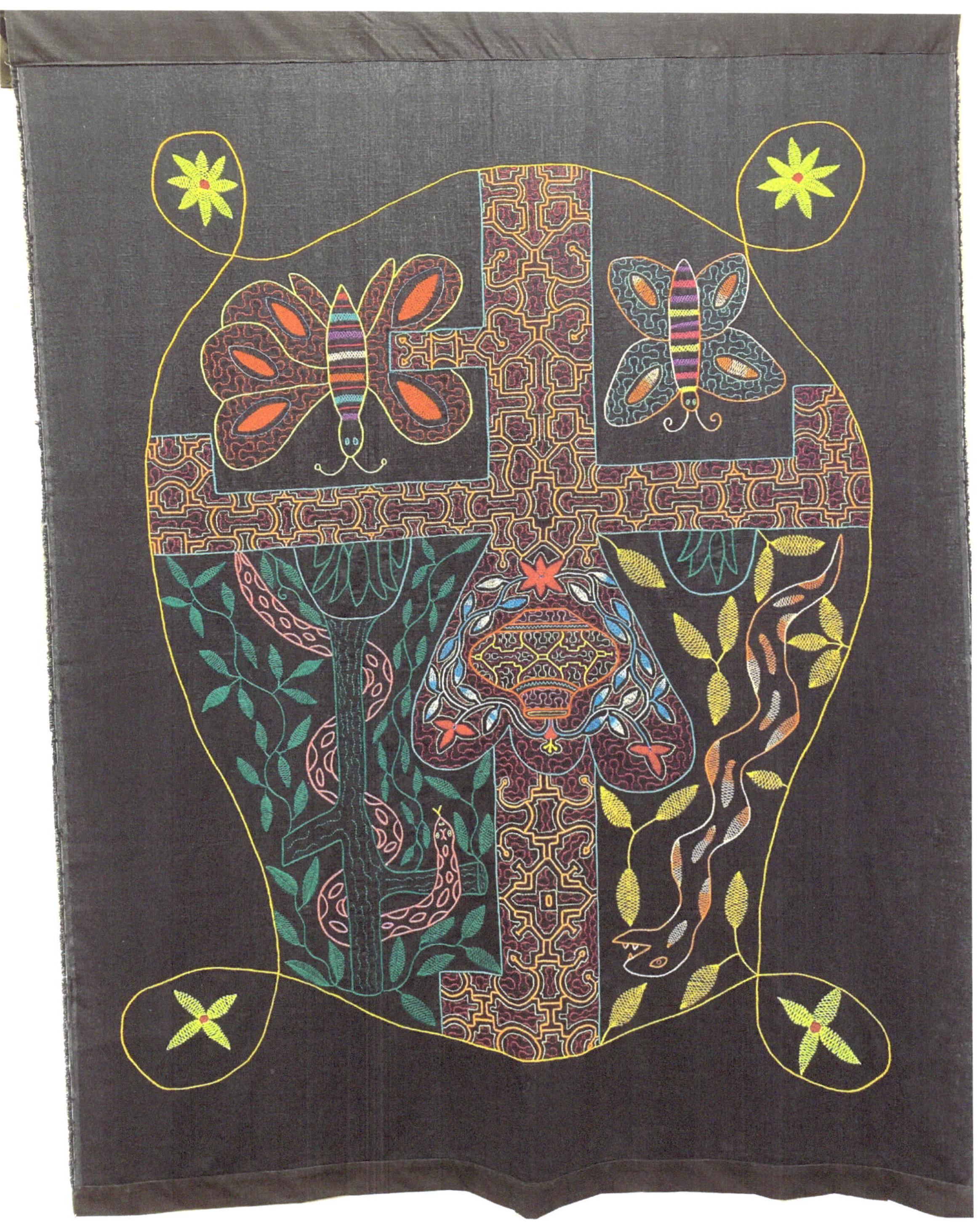

Courtesy of the artist and Klaus von Nichtssagend Gallery

Gail Thacker

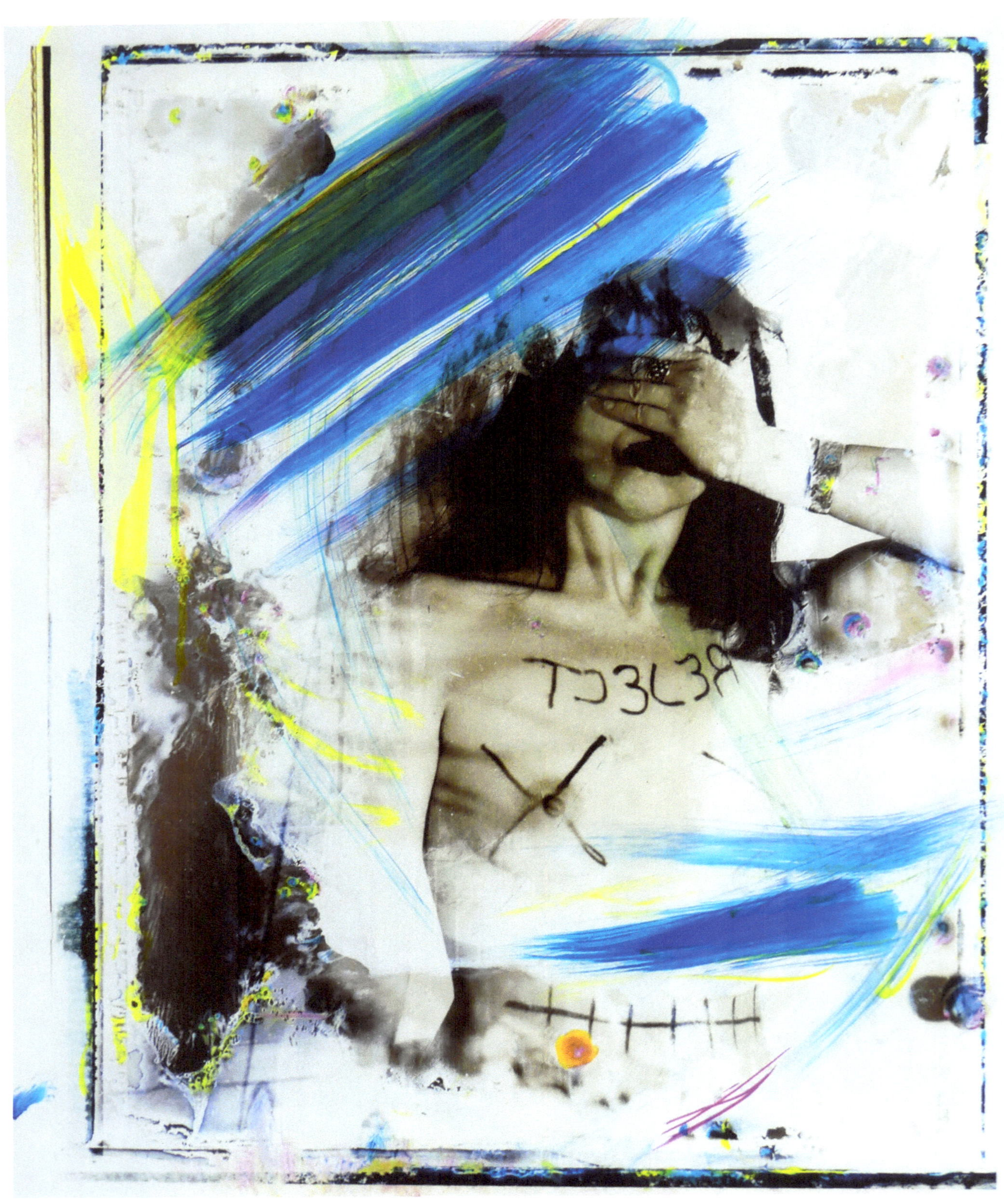

Self Portrait Reject 1996/2021
Polaroid anologue unique c print, paint & ink.
Courtesy of Howl Arts, NYC

An Underpass

I wonder if on several occasions
I was met by a Sondergeist who
Talked to me about you, invited me
To dine in San Georgio, take cognac
Against the wall of climbing vines—
Or, as I suspected, her letters
Of credentials were clandestine.
Call me infallible, passpartout,
Call me imprinted, fading in a circle-
Dance reading proofs, improbable,
An escutcheon proper with time—
I am Helvetiae, after all, and we don't
Understand why good luck is smooth
And unobtrusive, we barely believe
A single exuberance, and yet,
We're obliged and obligé, a long-range
Goal but a syncopated music.

       Only now summer knows who contracted
       The disease. Another reign begins
       Soon, says Mister X. Hopefully we'll be
       Out by then, and the world, without
       Knowing it will be someone like us.
       Not one of the best, but better, still.
       Observe the crows and the infinite
       Pleasures, absorb the past times—
       There's no magic; we're simply with-
       Drawn in the dark, feeling our hands
       And our hair, trusting that honor and
       Its pivot and its shade of sub-
       Stance—"Take no notice," the winged
       Celestial says. "Nobody's ever seen it.
       Existence is possible deep in the knees.
       Even the sound of trees can be
       Enlightening. Scrub the floor.
       Clear the woods of all intruders."
       How many bipeds does it take to make a planet?

Dawn's Early Light

have at it, the scraps, no matter, your move's lateral
built on your backs' then treat youse like filthy animals,
ritual killing, savages, urban cannibals
lethal lead levels, making your brain malleable
served with a stench, feasting on your own feces
demonic hellbent, reptilian species
caged generations, hunt and prey your offspring,
turn the light out, that moment when it go(es) bing
like the furor's experiments, just, not only on the jews
media framework, fuels the fake news
fillers for nutrients, inferior schools
concerns for your benefit, truly just a rouse
the focus is their agenda, control, and to abuse
the power that they've taken, our children is who they use
forced separation, family bond breaking
cheap forms of labor, is what there's high stakes in

Tamos

Estamos bien, pero vamos para mejor
logrado lo que no se compra, respeto y honor
con tiempo se realizado cuáles son de verdad
y lo que es mas importante, familia y comunidad
misericordia de Dios, y buena voluntad
buenas intenciones, bendiciones y piedad
por tó lo que hemos hecho que nos perdonara (ojalá)
solo la oportunidad, a corregir y mejorar
a la nueva generación poder le educar
abriendo le los ojos, con la fuerte realidad
arrepentimiento por tantos que han sufridos
bien agradecido por juicio que e aprendido
un mensaje pá los que hasen y los quienes tan cogido
los en camino de perdidos, especialmente a los chiquitos
cuales estan en mal hechos parece de competencia
pa' que verán que no ay futuro en la vida de delincuencia

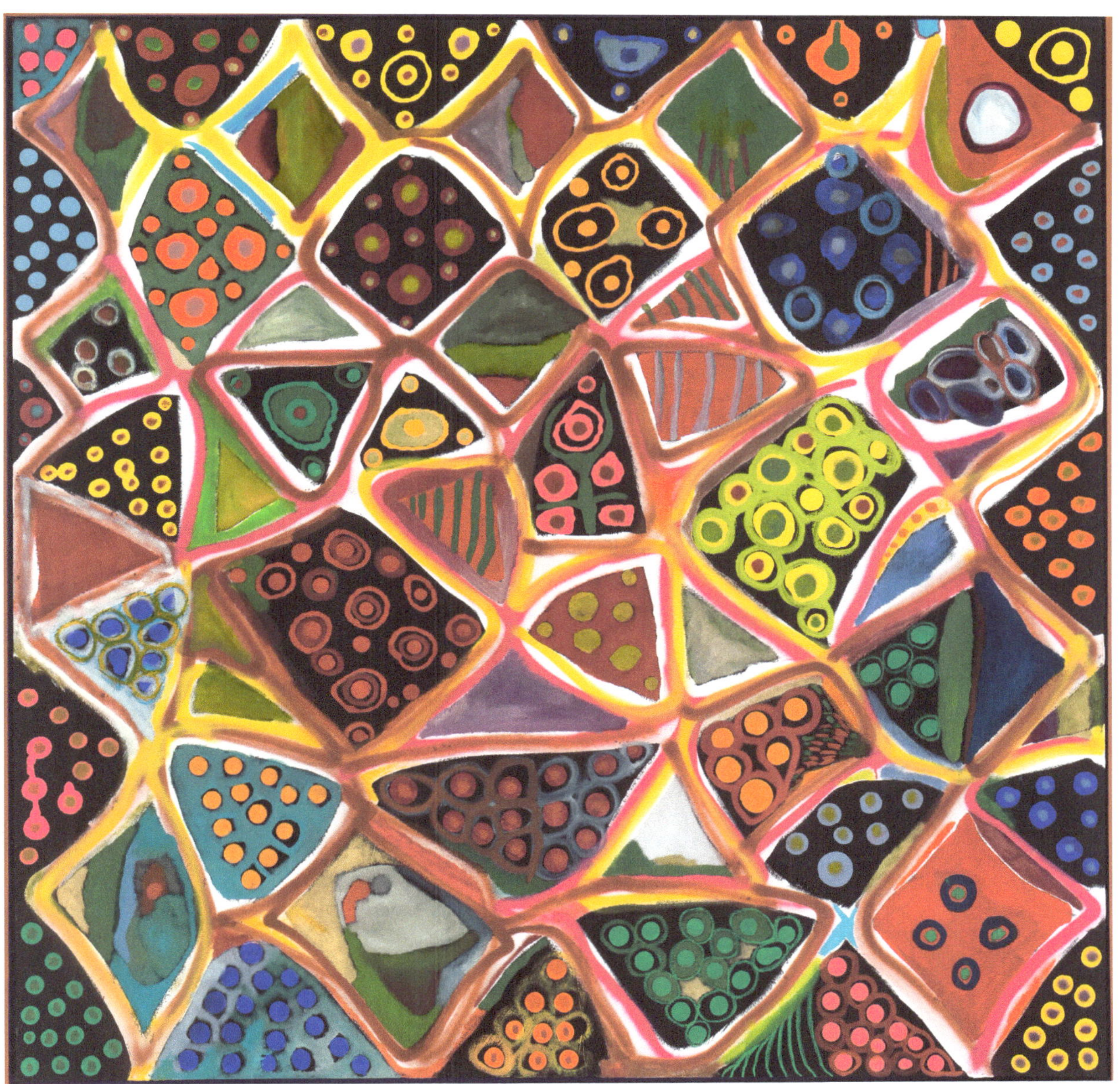

Malaria Tripping. Courtesy Nicola Vassell Gallery

John Casquarelli

All Poets Welcome

For Lewis Warsh

He calls me into his office, gives me
a copy of *The Origin of the World* and
Our Friends Will Pass Among You Silently.

I stare at his bookshelves, half-listening.
He smiles and I recognize it's possible to
dream without sleeping. This must be how
a tiger feels when it becomes aware of its stripes.

On paper, growls are fragments, each stanza
a grain of dust in an hourglass. His gray sweater
includes threads of second generation
St. Mark's Poetry Project Wednesday readings.

"Take my long poem workshop and read
the archived letters of New York School poets
at Fales Library. I'll grant you access."

The pen hums. Outside, Washington Square radiates
with skateboards and dancing lights at dusk.
One day, I'll give these moments names, place them
in a Mason jar, and they will be inseparable.

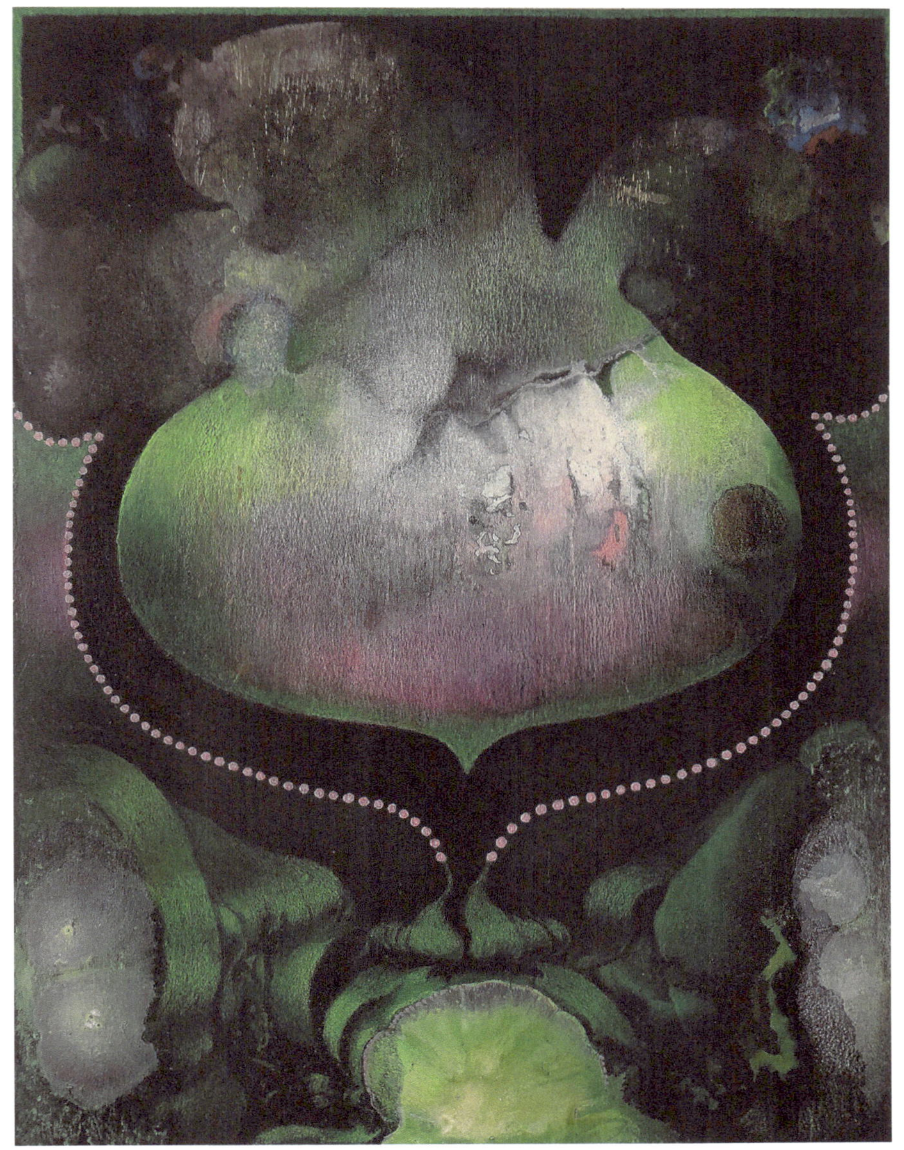

Phantom Root 2019
ink, acrylic, colored pencil on wood
12 x 10 in.

Elizabeth Guthrie

Revolution

It takes one revolution
A vertigo
Like seeing the sun revolving
Around the planets
To lose you

To find you
The wave of your hand
At the end of an exchange
Set in motion by an evolution
Of places suddenly by a turn

Of events I am the woman
Staggering across the street
With the shopping cart full
Of empty cans and bottles in front

Of gaping drivers so swollen
At any moment any of us
And suddenly like the planetarium
Show the heavenly realigned
To shift our view of places

To a space where
I am the man in front of the drug
Store asking with his eyes just
Asking at just the right time

As seeing that I would give him all
That I have to ease this suffering
Of our bodies and hearts whirling
A solo melody rising out
Of the music of the spheres

Hand in Hand

I can't let go.
There has been such
a large handful of them.

Let them go
rolling over
and over

some with some sides
bright and some
blistered.

I can't
let them
bounce, my handful

pressed open in some
parts a finger against
an open handful.

over each and touched
each over other let such
a large handful go

blistered in between
letting go and bounce hold
between the bounce

(I can't let go.)

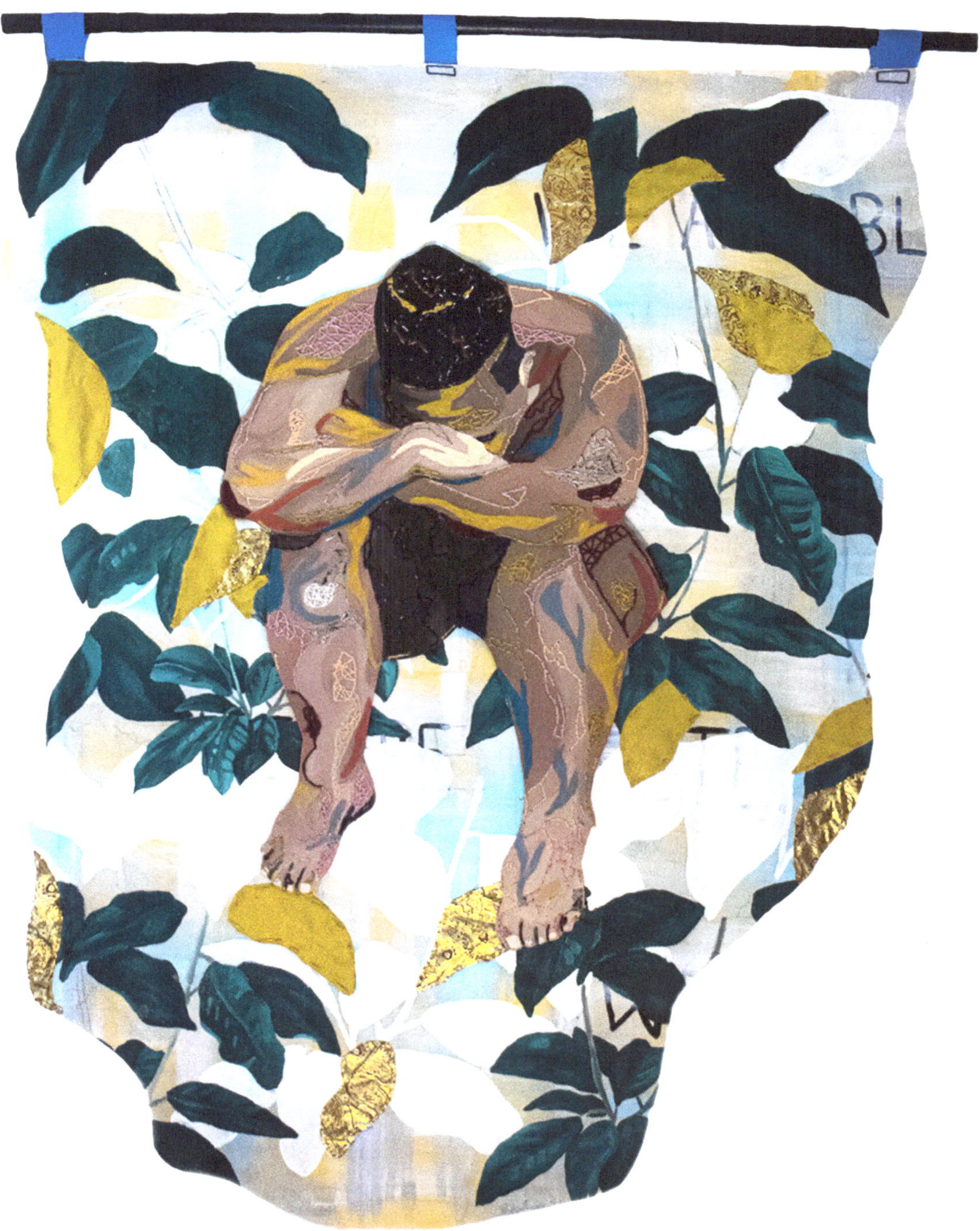

Rise, acrylic, fabric, yarn, dowel rod, and wood cutout 51.5 x 48 in.
Courtesy of Latchkey Gallery, NYC

Maria Damon & Alan Sondheim*

A Word of Unknown Origin

Less auteur please
lizard-like conditions [attack by]
"lizard people"? [they deserve your vote]
lizards are endangered
and busy flashing the most
~~blues reds~~ because "colorless" in the next
line leads to an exclusivity.
colorless lumen with puff-streaks for the
color-blind like myself, a true storey,
the fourth where I sometimes lived
while elsewhere now
averaging deaths
700 per day
orbs of red hauteur **however**
our Saviour's blood was red,
type *O* like the Story and not thereupon to be
desecrated, and did He not live
in the within the Red Confinations of
Providence, and not among the
(less please yes)
emollients of New York
don't get any big ideas please
emolument phase please
Orm's Ormulum Alarum
where we have collapsed
with Him as with a star that, it
seems, may release a six-pointed nuclear
explosion unfathomable,
generating
molecular gold and radioactive
elements, O Yes, Please, Yes, Please,
Yes, Minister, Yes, Prime! Minister,
yes pleas an innovative
branding technique
without rhythmic magic
a shimmering red
like ~~gilded~~ blood
on the white lily pleasing only
Him, Trumpeting His Own
Replacement Apocalypse (H.O.R.A.)
A sacred union, pleated in dance.

"bold, hardy," from PIE root *kar- "hard." Beekes finds likely
from "mouse"), so called because the (Modern French lzard), from
Latin -art, from Old French -ard, -art, English, as in buzzard,
drunkard. French and English is probably German and Dutch used as
a Latin lacertum "upper arm, Latin musculus "a muscle," Old
French laisarde "lizard" Pre-Greek. Proto-Germanic *-hart/*-hard
The German element is from a word pattern similar to that of
added to it" [Johnson], late also arm-muscle or the lizard, is as
an mouse" (diminutive of mus bastard, Latin sense, the became a
living It is identical to bracchium), which suggests a 14c.,
element in common nouns, and thus from German -hard, -hart
"hardy," hardly in many personal names, often used influenced
Movement of the biceps intensifier work-it work-it, but in Middle High
is unclear Which element in lacertus (fem. lacerta) "lizard," likertizein
"to jump, dance," literally "little "an animal lusarde, from
Anglo-French lusard, muscular part of the arm, from the original.
De Vaan finds the passing into Middle English in pejorative by
words in -ard. of resembling a serpent, with legs shape and
coward, blaffard ("one shoulder to the elbow" (opposed to unknown
origin. The ending in were thought to resemble mice or mouses. It
which forming the second element who stammers"), etc. A back-
formation too abysmal to express —It thus words
perhaps connected to Greek as it doth creep across the page
rightwardly descendant in secular scholastica

am I the only one recognizes that if you take (the word) "Latin"
and remove the L you get "atin" or "at in" as in I'm "at in Hell"?
or that if you take "animal" and reverse it, remove the L (AGAIN!!
- the "L"!!!) you get "anima"? What is "at in anima LL"? I am
positive the reference is to "atonement" in "Hells" (or the El, a
popular name for an elevated railway) (somewhat the same as we
fall towards a gushing end among the applecarts below). Hells,
Halls, Hills, Hulls, but the Holes and Wholes, one filling the other.
DO YOU SEE WHERE I AM GOING, DO YOU? It's like this:
Qanon = Kanon = Cannon; one queues for the El, does one **knot?**
Oh and by the way I'm the first to point out, I am sure that LIVE
is EVIL backwards, that DOG is GOD, that VILE and VEIL are
in there somewhere. Speaking of Diogenese lacertus, D. Lizard,
- note there is no relationship at all and THAT is the relationship.

NOW:

~~t if you tke (the word) "Ltin"~~

~~ke (the word) "Ltin"~~

~~tin"~~
~~m I the only know recognizes th~~

Vincent Katz

Placitas

spaces are deceptive
those cows look so small
there's a tree out there
"that stump must be
a thousand years old!"

clump of trees coming up
pendant road, RR track
more mesas in the distance
I'll miss this space
Springer 1 mile

I'm liking these trees a lot
Wow, that was Springer
Eagle Nest, Red River, Angel Fire
two new greens, one light, one dark
didn't make Placitas this time

Witness

A long look down the side
Nothing accumulates, sputters
A delinquent treason symbolizing
Foregone witness, forest murmur

That walk transformed winter
Or winter transforms looks
Aside from fashion, cut of pant
Another pharmacy out of order

Order and progress fight to prove
One song on radio can still speak
Neon begins the day as ways
Struck into probable armor

A New Year

4:15 lights in park not yet on streets
January warm chilling women men walk
curving path through center zone Alphaville
city someday will rest my head
square reachable bell's hazy hours
gaunt facades hardly changed decades
massive trunks neon aglined squirrels sport
lightness shade sky descending HOTEL
half moon half building over gilt top leers
man limps lawn squirrel silhouette
down branch above building back
meet third almost to Metropolitan
circle clock face now fourth and fifth
bench snap foreign photographs

4:25 street lights still not on park lights
significant walk jacketless limbs
flannel circle January park colder
night infiltrates appear lights
thought shifts squirrel husk to pavement
figures astride Appellate Divison marble
J. B. Lord Architect C. T. Wills Builder
A. D. MCM allegory 1998 new year
mosaic warmth wood massive
hokey murals hint deviant sadistic
arrows whips prostrate nudes
garbage truck melody keeps warm
penetrates sanctioned rejuvenated
back across square where left off

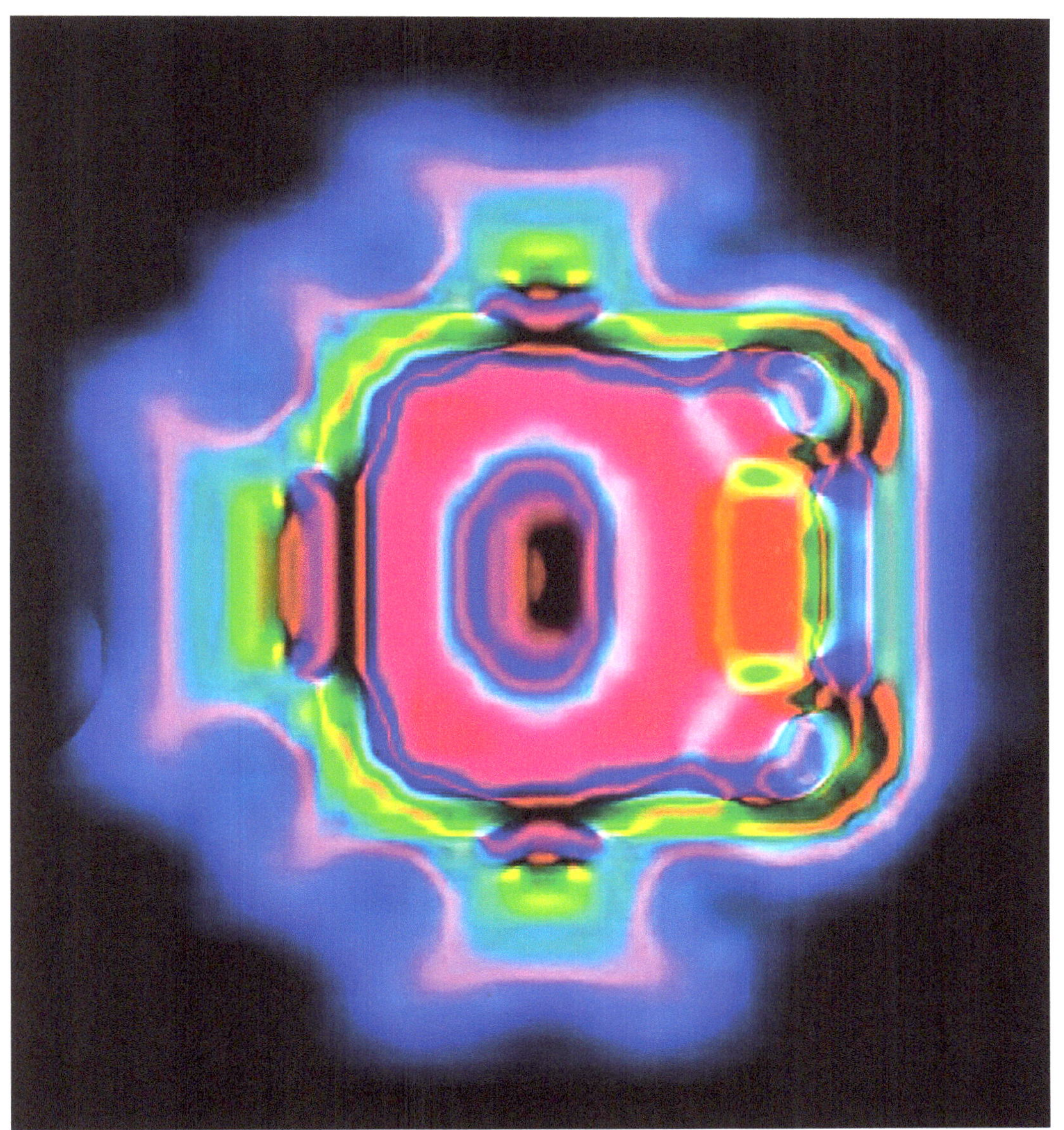

Molly Glow Available as an NFT with additional video object.

Robert Hershon

CHATTER

I did the Saturday puzzle on Sunday and
the Sunday puzzle on Saturday and I
watched a thousand hours of cops and robbers
when my friend assigned me the task of writing
a baseball poem, since right now there is no
baseball except in memory so I thought of
the Miracle Mets and then the Boys of Summer
but they both seemed frayed from overuse and I
began to think of the teams of my boyhood, call them
the Boys of Early Spring—Eddie Stanky and Pete Reiser
and Cookie Lavagetto, Kirby Higbe and Ed Head and that perfect
baseball name, Dixie Walker, brother to Harry the Hat Walker,
and remembered more as a bigot who wouldn't play with Jackie Robinson
than as an outfielder, but I didn't know that when I was
ten and we had the only television set at 946 Bushwick Avenue
and I watched the games by myself with a bag of candy corn
the cheapest loose candy Woolworth's sold, assuming
the Dodgers and I would grow old together (twelve, fourteen, beyond)
and wondering why all baseball announcers had Southern accents
and now the rich players and the even richer owners have finally
decided to play some baseball and I guess I'll slump down and
stare at the games, by myself again, but without candy corn

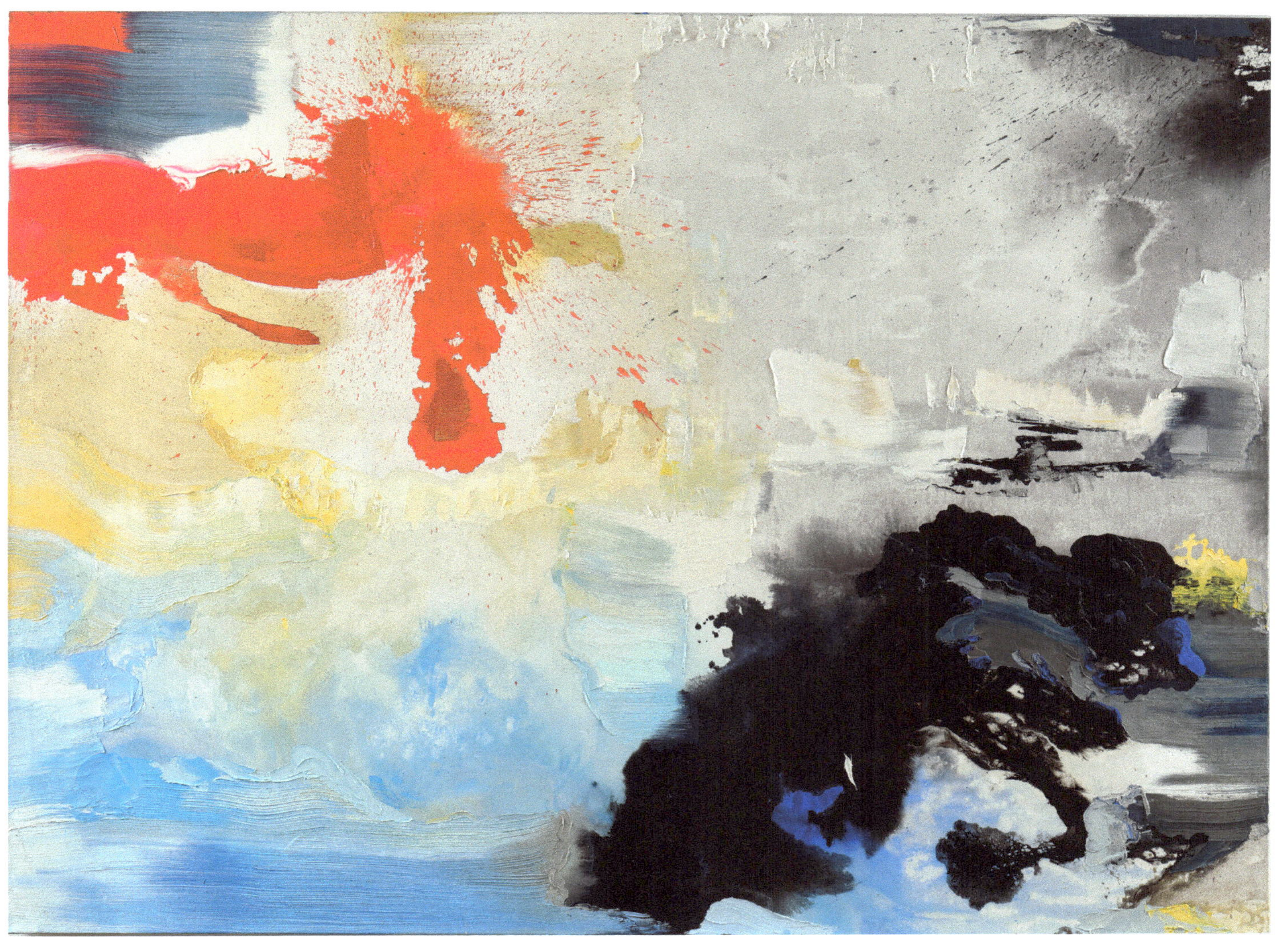

Tales from the Underground 2006 pigment, medium, oil on canvas 83 x 111 in. Photo: Jean-Baptiste Béranger

Arden Wohl

Sulzberger on Vacation

Sulzberger on vacation
at mercy of zombie editor
sleepwalking past the row of soda can tabs
like a daisy chain
the contour(s) of infinity
each structure primarily maintained by
the profilers
mounds that raise the embankment
buildings without power
children trading
teenagers pickin' the weeds

the concrete bandshell silhouettes
my friend's AA meeting
while we all stand reticent

forget the storm surge
at the core of it
the foundation
the cornerstone
with a sick nucleus

ok, enough with the outlines

the substance is water
and it mixes with
Screed

in the business of garbage?
can you make sense of the fallow surplus?

I will hold your contract

spill the debris and make another fresh kill
You sign it and sentence

so am I an outlier or a seed blowing on the
East River?
refusing to transplant
sloppily, slipping between establishments

oh how I hate order and
pArtOcracy
Just let me die in the red tape

bury me in the contaminant-filled meadow
just a few blocks from La Mama

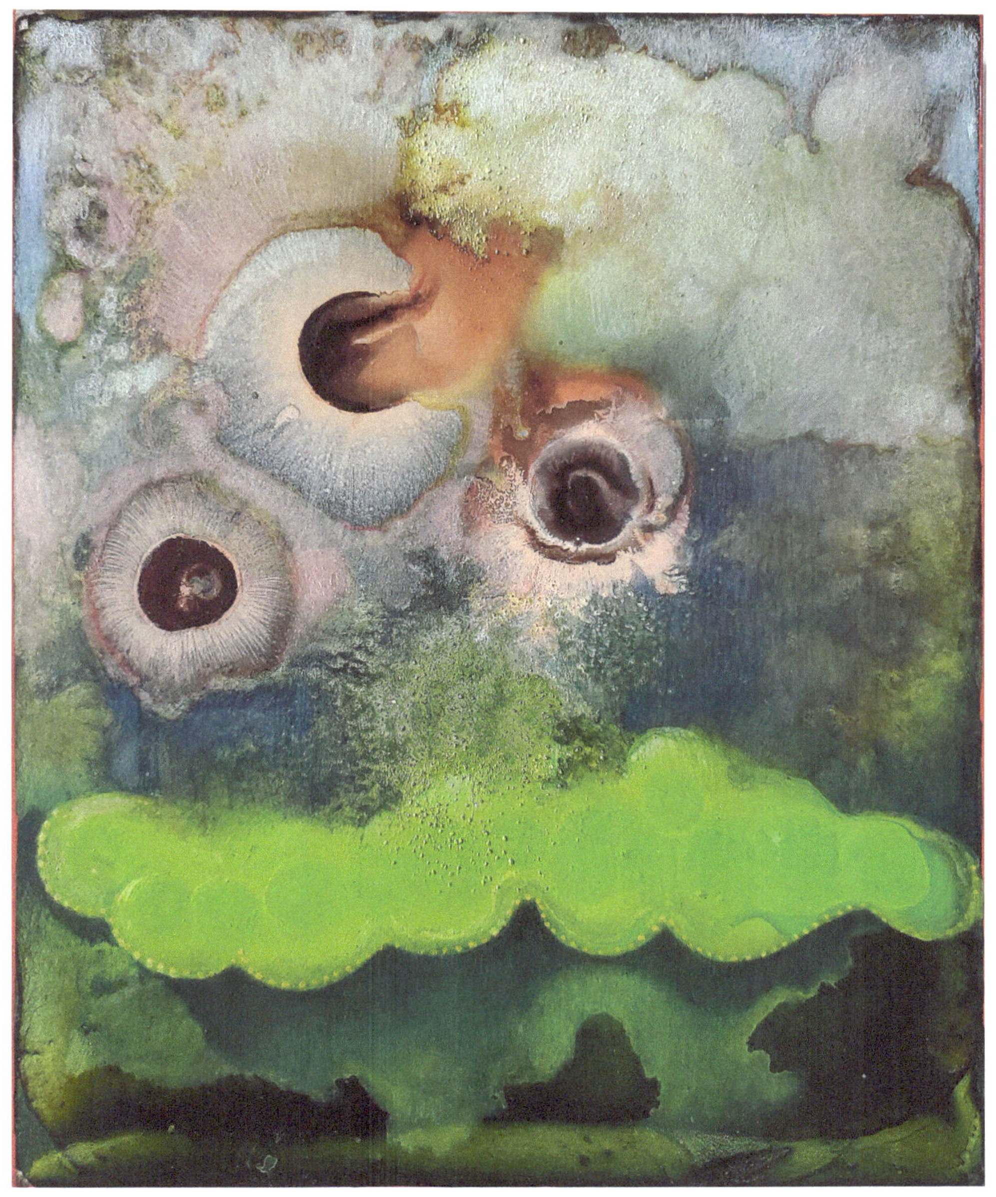

Acid Mammatus 2019
Ink, acrylic, gouache, colored pencil on panel
10 x 8 in.

Eileen R. Tabios

The Edges of Flesh Are Not Straight

After *Crystal Landscape Painting (Mountains)* by Josiah McElheny

Wasn't it Baudelaire
who could only feel
the significance of sky
by jailing its expanse
between the edges
of parallel skyscrapers?

Manhattan might throw
up glass buildings
but can't avoid the grey
interruptions of steel
scaffolding, no matter how
thin, as if steel can mimic air.

Thus, Dear Sapphire Sky—
dim yourself to accommodate
the light within four walls
offering a home, new to you
but a compromise you accept
because objects can be touched.

Converse with the light behind
your sudden triangles because
objects can be shaped. The light
manifests as slim glass pyramids.
Note how its air lacks scars—
how it welcomes the transformation
of image into a physical relationship

so intimate it leaves the wall
to become three-dimensional
for you

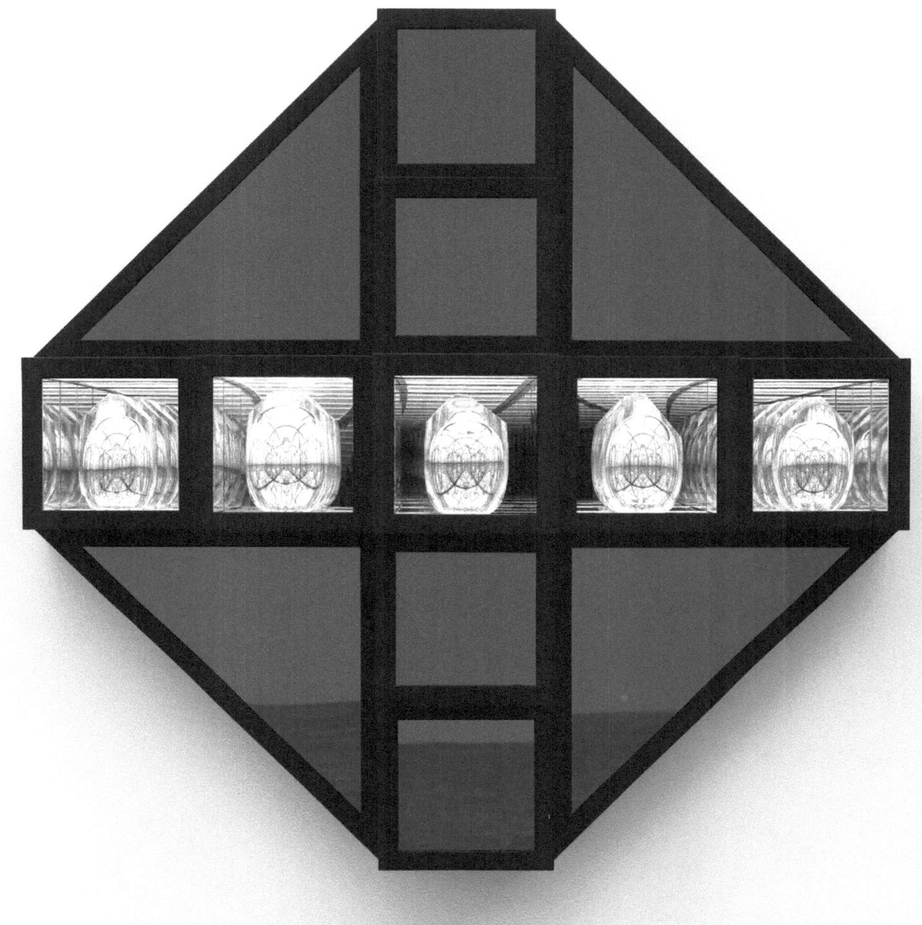

Crystal Landscape Painting (Mineral), 2019
Hand-blown cut, polished and mirrored glass, transparent and low-iron mirror, painted steel,
electric lighting and hardware 54 15/16 x 54 15/16 x 18 11/16 in., 139.5 x 139.5 x 47.5 cm. 350 lbs
Courtesy of the artist and James Cohan, Corbett vs. Dempsey, White Cube.

Adeena Karasick

From EICHA II: The Book of Lumenations

And in the ache of asylum

I have bent my bow
framed in the anchor of candied dalliance —

screaming in strung shadows, revenance

where limning sutures, festooned in sunshift

Lie with me
in the illicit quiver
of knotted conscience

Languish
through whispered harbors'

pressed exile
among evening's inheritance;

the providence of slipped

semes slants
sucking twilight

of latticed scatter

From EICHA III: The Book of Lumenations

Sheltered in netted inlets
of ripped dyssemia, fleshy sequiturs, wisteria, the taste of broken bans—

Hail the billow of campy siege, the truance of gilded travaille

And make me dwell in the darkened wreckage of feverish dread

In the censored resonance of pliant heaves;

The plated shudder of my parade.

Burn me in the binding bias in torqued harrow.

For I am woke in the swindled aperture of fibrous light;

And I am giddy with shaded want in the quiescence of ludic clues

Naked with his yoke in my mouth

Let him sit sultry for he has laid upon me

Let him put his mouth into the dust

Offer his shackles to the smitten

Let him be filled with peaches

From EICHA IV: The Book of Lumenations

And as care curls / in her swirled whorl's
spurred leurre / stirred
spur of porous roar

whose flayed fray forêts
flurried fury fiery folly

flares in the florid lore
of soaring horror

in the ripped wrought
raw lot

And in the raging contagion
of the yoked hurrah
we are riddled in thick drift
and drunk with iniquity—

asking whose balletic thirst
is clasped
in the synonymy

of our yaysay, purer than sinew, and wet with dusk
ruddier than choral, sapphire, milking crimson syrups
sifted riffs of spilt surfeits

Whose skin a

buttered vortex of fruited
folds fluted affinities
of ripened whim

crowned in syllabic aberrance

Eve Packer

12.15.20 7:58pm

for sparrow, i guess

the amoebas
of hope
rounding the door,
            mermaids of sorrow
sprinkle slam/dunk the ocean
floor, pinocchios of
            hopscotch
            pole-vaulting/ red (neon)
light
        when i was young i used
to wear a red
            dress no
            no garters no
snake/no problem

tues., 12.15.20: 8:07 pm

12.29.20

they say a new even more virulent strain
of corona
rampaging britain, and now in colorado,
so
for how long
can we hide just when at summer's end. thru fall,
we see some dangling party favors
hurtling thru the masked mist,
here comes a torpedo
ripping thru the PPE
of a happy healthy new year

tues, 12.29.20: 7:42 pm

new year's eve day: 4:09 pm

We used to toggle
from larry jones' loft
above the pyramid club, to
st mark's, later from nuyorican
to st mark's, last year, from
the church on christopher,
while the rest of the city
was in recovery we were doing
our slam-dunk punch drunk poetry crush—

i've never been a fan
of new year's eve, this year
the sky a lead zeppelin over
manhattan, i got to swim
that's a plus, i miss the bagels
and lox, i miss human spit & touch—

i miss you all so much

thurs., 12/31/20: 4:21 pm

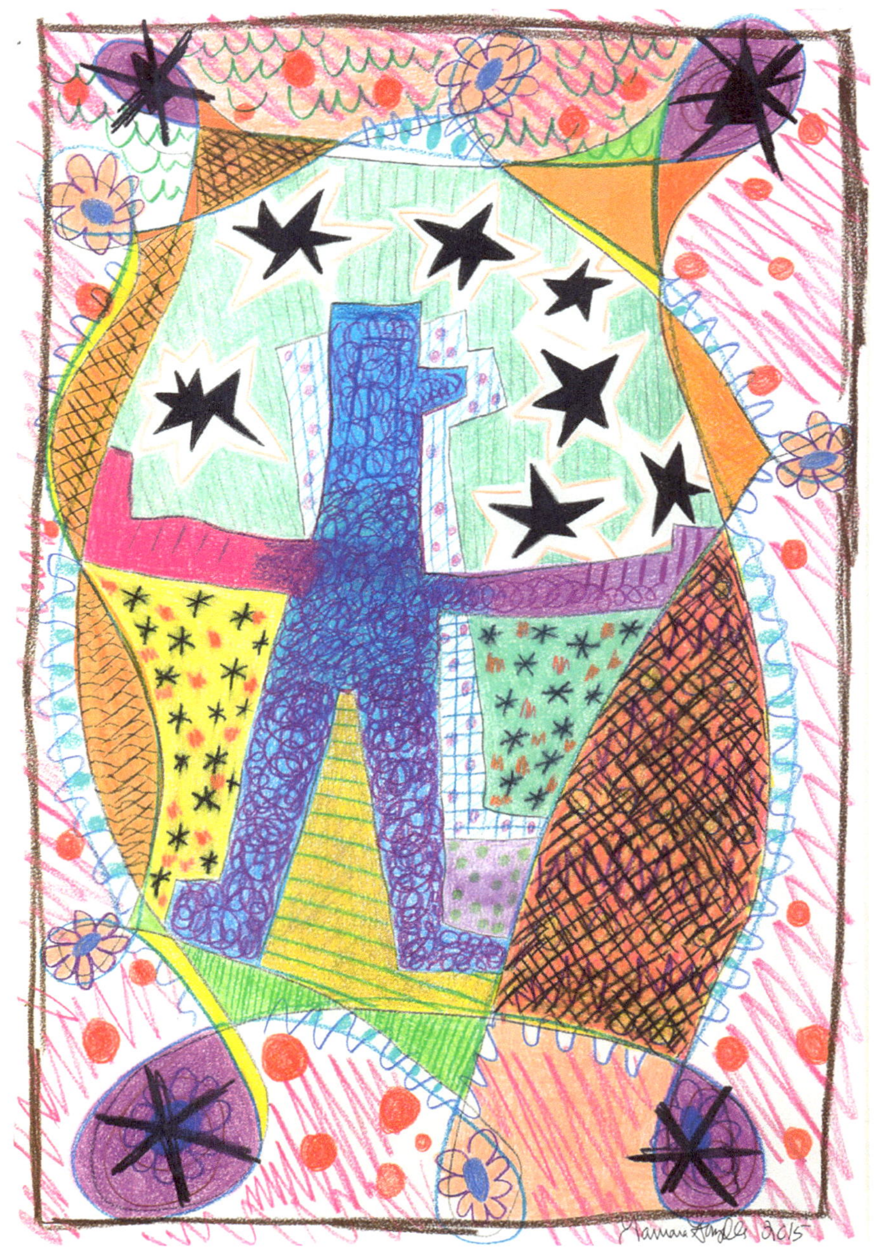

Courtesy of the artist

Julie Evans

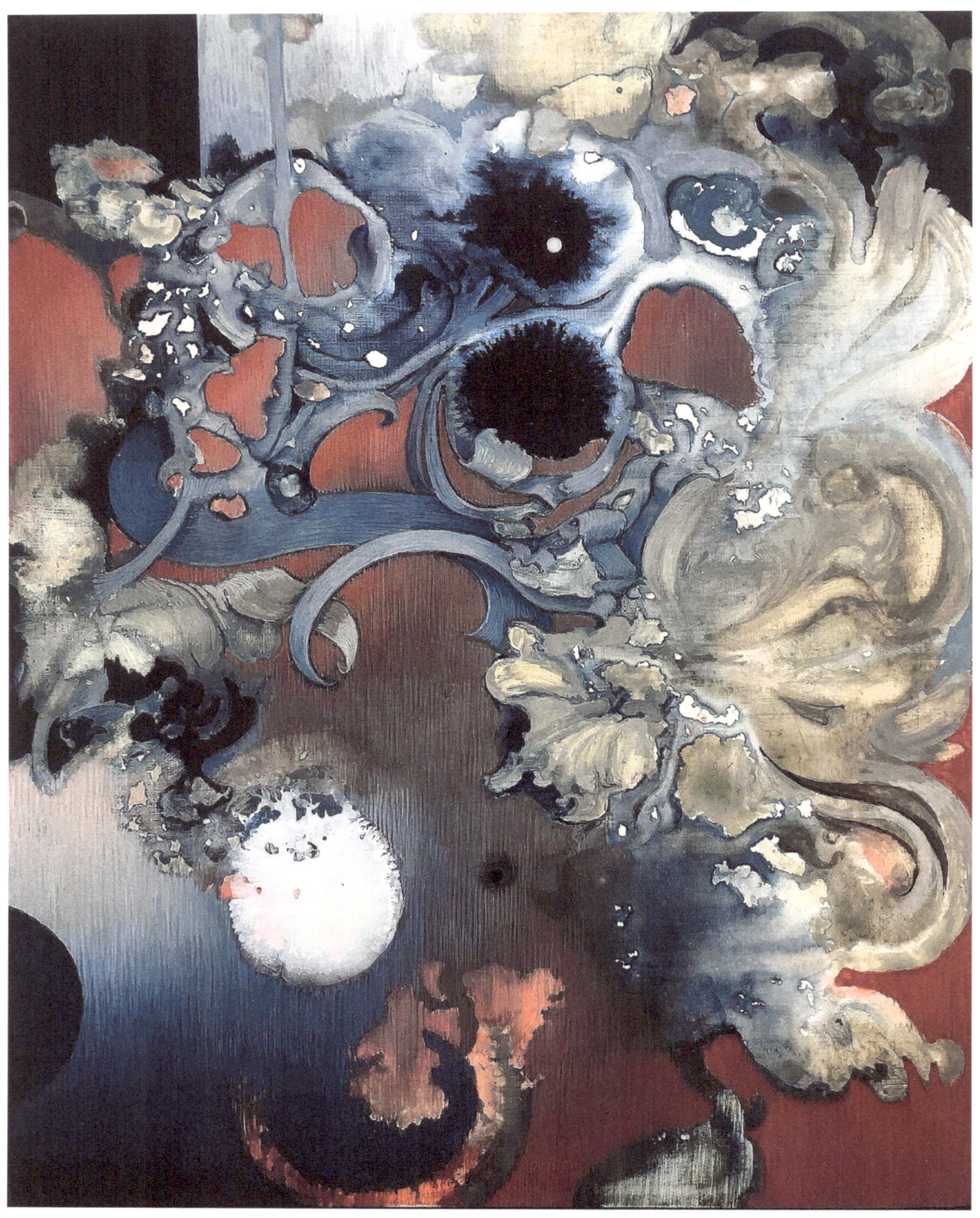

Unscreen 2019 ink and gouache on wood 14 x 11 in.

JOY OF COOKING

the last line is often the hardest
unless it writes itself
at which point darkness
has its little moment in the sun
and then it's closing time at the end of history
approximately

which is to say there is an opening
and then it closes
forever and a moment

mortality grips us with mortality tongs
here a pinch of compassion
there a yelp of suffering so close
to the cries of birth
or desire coming through the light
with eyes closed

one must take to heart the joy
of cooking and keep in mind
the mixed blessing in forgetting
which creates each new day
by stirring up old souls in new bodies
or vice versa and venturing forth
as the crow flies past our vision
into the ineffable

there is strange consolation in knowing
that what we know will never be enough
to silence the enigma at our core
and that in time we may be asked to revere
that about which we know nothing

still there is always the next something
to distract us like a gray tilted fedora
in a window or the last line of a poem
which is often the hardest
unless it writes itself

Mike DeCapite

From *Jacket Weather*: Radiator

I missed her before dawn with the radiators coming on.

*

After three days of media hysteria over the coming blizzard, after they pronounced it historic in advance and called it the blizzard of the century, after all the canceled flights and closed airports and chains on the bus tires, after the supermarkets sold out of bread including the honey-nut whole-grain English muffins and toaster-ready corn cakes and Portuguese festival spelt loaf, and after the bodegas sold out of bottled water including every last bottle with a label printed in Cyrillic, you know what happened? It snowed. Yes, on Saturday night it snowed, and Sunday we walked up Fifth Avenue through the slush moats at every curb, and I wound up in a boyfriend chair at Lord & Taylor.

*

White-topped water towers on a white sky. The snow is whiter by the minute, in contrast to the sky. There's no such thing as time, and the world is yours. Snow white on grey sky.

*

green Brussels-sprout leaves in a white sink

*

The radiators clank, and hiss, and bang, and hiss.

*

I sat in this room as it got dark. I didn't pick up a book or a magazine. Didn't get dinner started. Just sat on the couch, looking out the window. The sun had got below the cloud ceiling and chosen the Empire State and Chrysler Buildings and a band of apartment buildings, which stood in a dark blue sky transmitting now a burning auspicious gold, now vermilion. At 5:00 the lights at the top of the Chrysler Building started in quick increments like the opening of a fan, and soon the others, only just now red, had given up the ghost, gone dull, and left me with the feeling of a drug wearing off, returning me to my senses and time's flow, and it was just another night.

From *Jacket Weather*: Three Views from One Window

Saturday afternoon at the Vermeer, reading on the bed. I keep looking up from the book to the outside wall, with its window reflecting water towers and rooftops and sky. A view like an old linen postcard. Read another page or two. Back to that window, and those cutouts climbing against the sky in jumbled reds, blonds, and browns, doubled in the glass, no weight, no mass, no movement. Pigeons.

*

Saturday afternoon, reading on the bed. My attention wanders from the page to the window outside ours, the water-tower skylines superimposed in rising ranks—dozens of water towers, and all the intricacies of a cityscape lit by the sun: facades, arched windows, cornices, cranes, scaffolding—row on row of these in the placid light, every detail registered on the glass plate. A world without mass, without time, without sound, dreaming itself all day in the glass. With a frame around it. One puff of rising steam.

*

Sunday I'm reading on the bed. In our neighbor's window the water towers are stacked in a lemongrey sky. All day the light doesn't change. All day a tea-kettle wind is whistling in the vents and the white slow plumes of steam are rising. All day I'm here reading—how many of those do you get in a year? In a lifetime? Late in the afternoon the sun comes out. And then the light gets dialed down and dialed down until, in a deep-blue sky, only a few silver rooftop pipes are still gleaming. Dialed down until there's one white water tower bobbing on a sea of night that's poured into the streets below, and those rooftop pipes are the gold of smoked sable.

Chris Lee

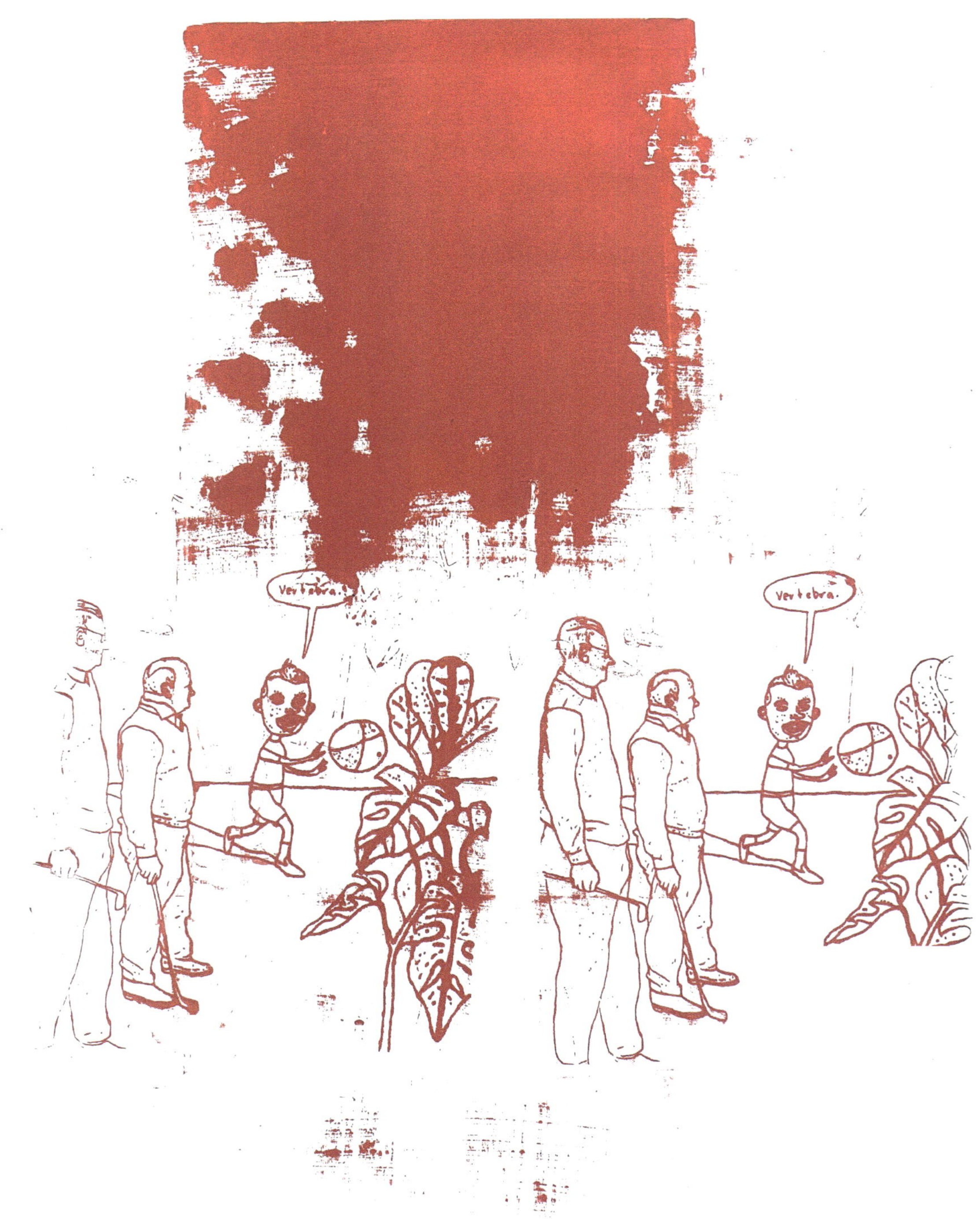

Untitled ink on vellum 2018

Another Beautiful Day in the Pandemic

The bumble bees are fat with honey
The humming birds hover like helicopters in the sun
The chipmunks skirt across the grass like racing cars
The cat watches the shadows play in the field of the lord
Another beautiful day in the pandemic

Cross my heart and hope to live
Grieve with me in the dark folds
Where memory plays out of tune tricks with Father Time
Where losers grin and winners
Spend all the money they own
And dancing girls twirl in the hot complacency of the sun
Another beautiful day in the pandemic

The garden is dense with the perspiration of morning
Pinks whistle—Reds purr
Blues rustle—Whites shimmer like stars
I'll take you in my arms and do-si-do
Where the truth rushes in like a fool
And trees stand tall against criminals
Snatching alibis from the branches of despair
Another beautiful day in the pandemic

Let's meet at the gates of Eden
Where fate is split like a rail
And love is thrown into the wind like apple seeds
Where clocks rust to oblivion
And the morning rises into the clouds
Like a silent prayer
For those who are lost
Another beautiful day in the pandemic

Suitcase

In the quiet time of evening
when the katydid's song ends
the moon still shines above.

She's packing her suitcase
what will she carry home?

Under the silent stars
investments made in
time multiply or they

can disintegrate by
astronomical charts
sent via email.

Everyone knows
you need to look up
to see the galaxy.

Friend Request

Politics on Facebook
filled with manipulation and lies
I can't play that game.
This public display-
show what you please,
fill your world with pretty pictures
or try to cure a disease.
Did somebody say
"Birthday Fundraiser Please?"
It's the Facebook parade.

Self-promotion free of charge
Who's in charge?
You can show me your nightmare
or put on a show, become a fantasy lover
who's to know?
Guaranteed personality upgrade.
What? Now you want to unfriend me?
What a tease!

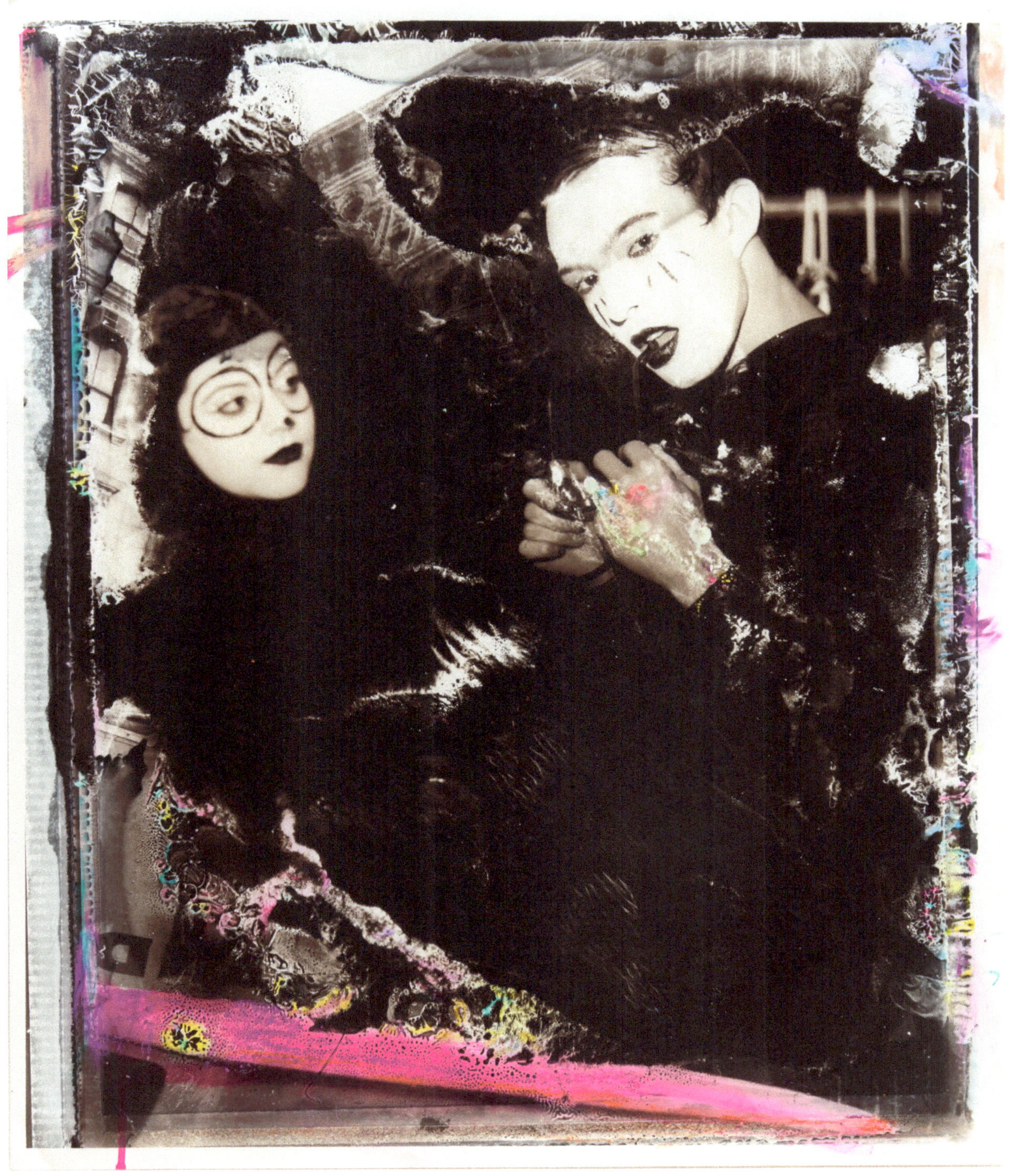

Shani & Francois The Libation Bearers 1999/2018
Polaroid anologue unique c print, paint & ink.
Courtesy of Howl Arts, NYC

Sevda Akyuz

little boy

—I—
fortune-teller:
your future has been revealed to you
                            my child
in your dreams

too bad
I don't remember them, ain't it

nobody has truly understood
your soul yet
                        mon petite

I already know that
          the question is
will they ever do

                    ma cherie
I see you've never had
          peace of mind
you should take it easy you know

I do

—II—
        she told our futures
five unalike women
        one by one
in a back room
where the baby sleeps
        fortunately
he was out at the time
        but I wonder
if all those ominous things said
lingered in the room with her
        cigarette smoke
to give the little boy
        nightmares later

SCARLET

Sorrowful is scarlet and its end
Scattered pieces from dead finch.
Clock strikes by a roadless side,
We get encircled as we circle our life.

Empty tummy, arid brain,
Mouths inside a lime pit
and busted is the feeling everywhere.
The wand that rendered our life
noble ran away unwanted.

Open spaces   widowed windows
                        will match no more,
Stars are frozen
                  on a scarlet lake.

SALAMANDER

In the hidden winters of water,
swims a blind salamander
                        for centuries long.

Every night knowing this
On a cave wall
A blue slave puts her shadow to sleep.

Mountains of the slave dance in the dark,
Just so wings remain a dream,
the slave remains sole on the same wall
and the salamander swims in its non-way.

Blind salamander!
Won't its hands get worn out groping?
Its eyeless head is sure to get yanked,
As its hands become eyes and its eyes hands.

*Translated from Turkish by Sevda Akyuz

Bill Considine

Cry Wolf

Off-moments, all akilter,
arms akimbo, trains of
almost thoughts sliding through
when snarls of a wolf pounce

from dark edging, a sleek, grey
predator, long teeth bared.
It rips and ravages
disjoints and smears a mess

subliminal passing as sublime
a glimpse of entrails
splattered on the floor.
They seem to spell wolf

but it's devoured and gone
and only I am howling.

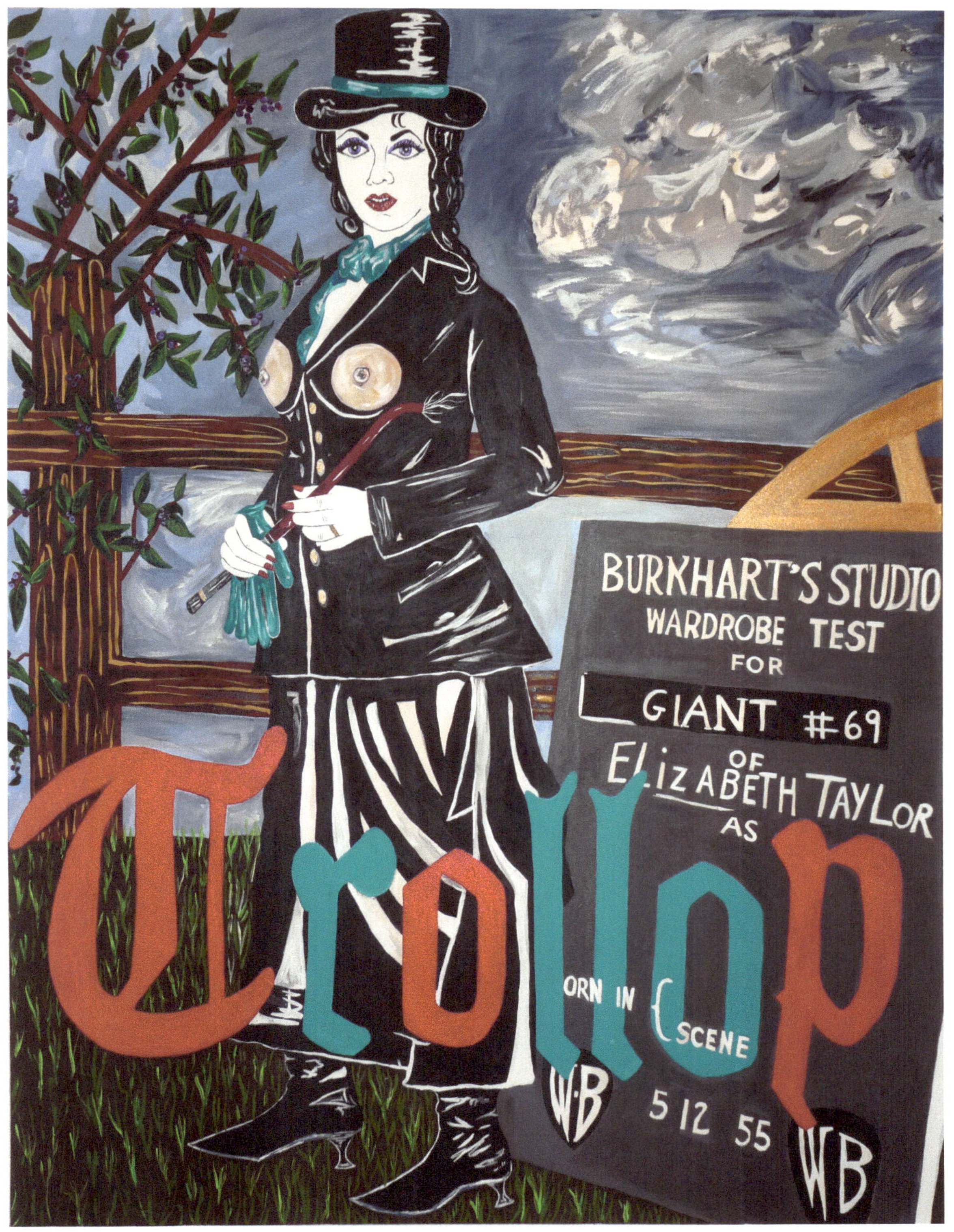

Trollop: from the Liz Taylor Series (Raintree County) 2012
Acrylic on canvas 78 x 58 in.

Jerelyn Hanrahan

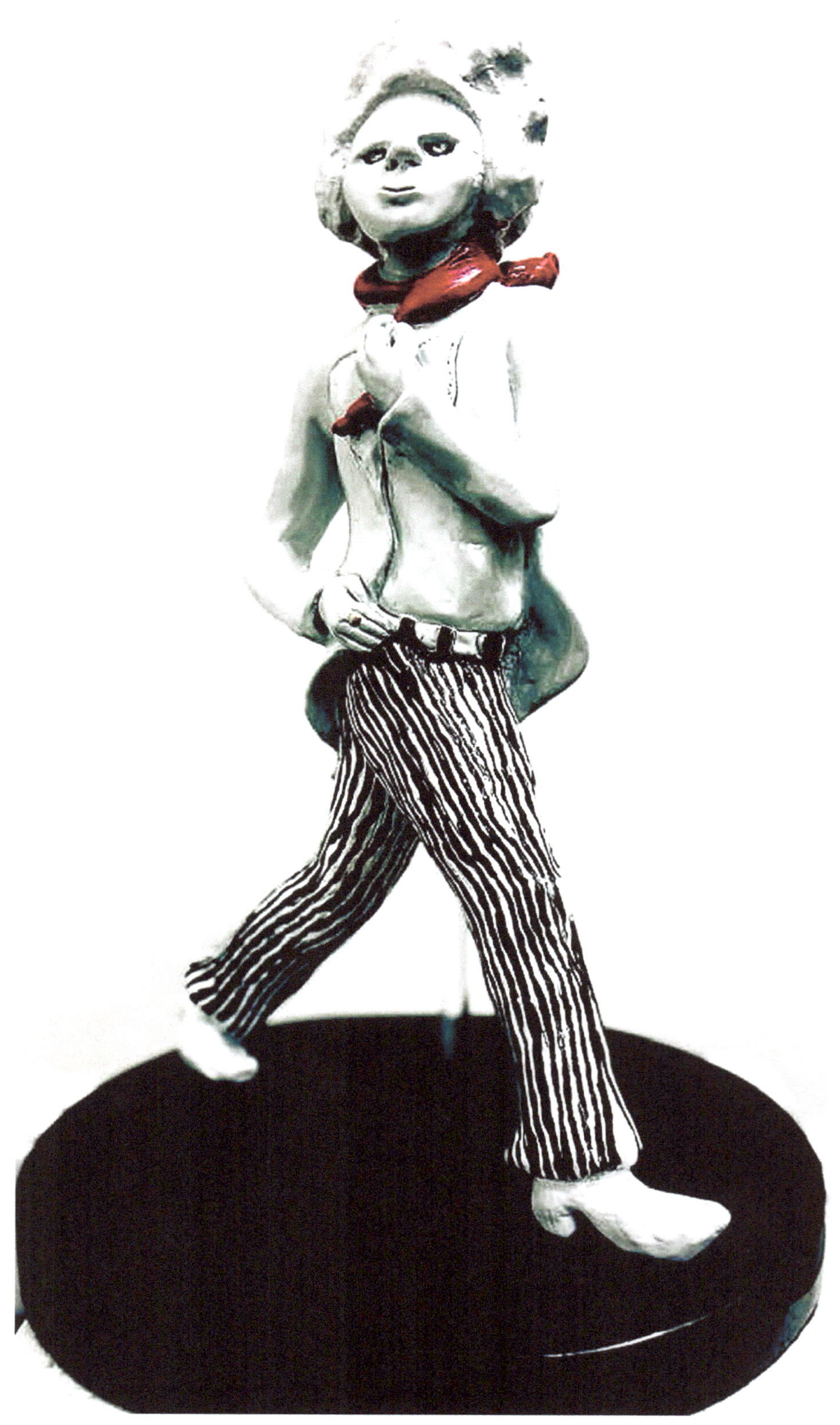

DUDE (LES) 2021 painted porcelain, granite base 12 x 12 x 20 in.

SWEEPSTAKE

Garlic paper flakes off like dried seconds
waiting for me to put words on them.
I whirl through the month, a dizzy twister.
Not every day is a holiday. You don't say?

A genie rises from the bowl. Smoke signals.
Coffee holds out a brown mitten.
We grind the candle light, smelting ardor.
An aqua tug bullies its cargo upstream.

Plenty to take care of here. Plenty to share.
Trains leave every hour but we stay.
Glinting wires hint at the unseen
guides that keep our act gliding on air.

The river slips from steel into teal satin.
Dusk's push broom comes, sweeping us on.

GHOST POWDER

A few clouds scallop the sky like pale fish
over the river. The carousel on Pier 25
closes for the season. I waste my days
courting puppets and chasing women.
October turns out its empty pockets,
squeezing the last glow from evening.

The nation teeters on spindly hind legs.
I almost lose it in the Bureau of Frustration.
Baz and I swap jail stories at Howl!
The pigeon lady quivers under feathers
at Union Square. Katherine Bradford
paints a pirate ship in my imagination.

Another friend had a stroke.
The frogs have a motto: "Born to croak."

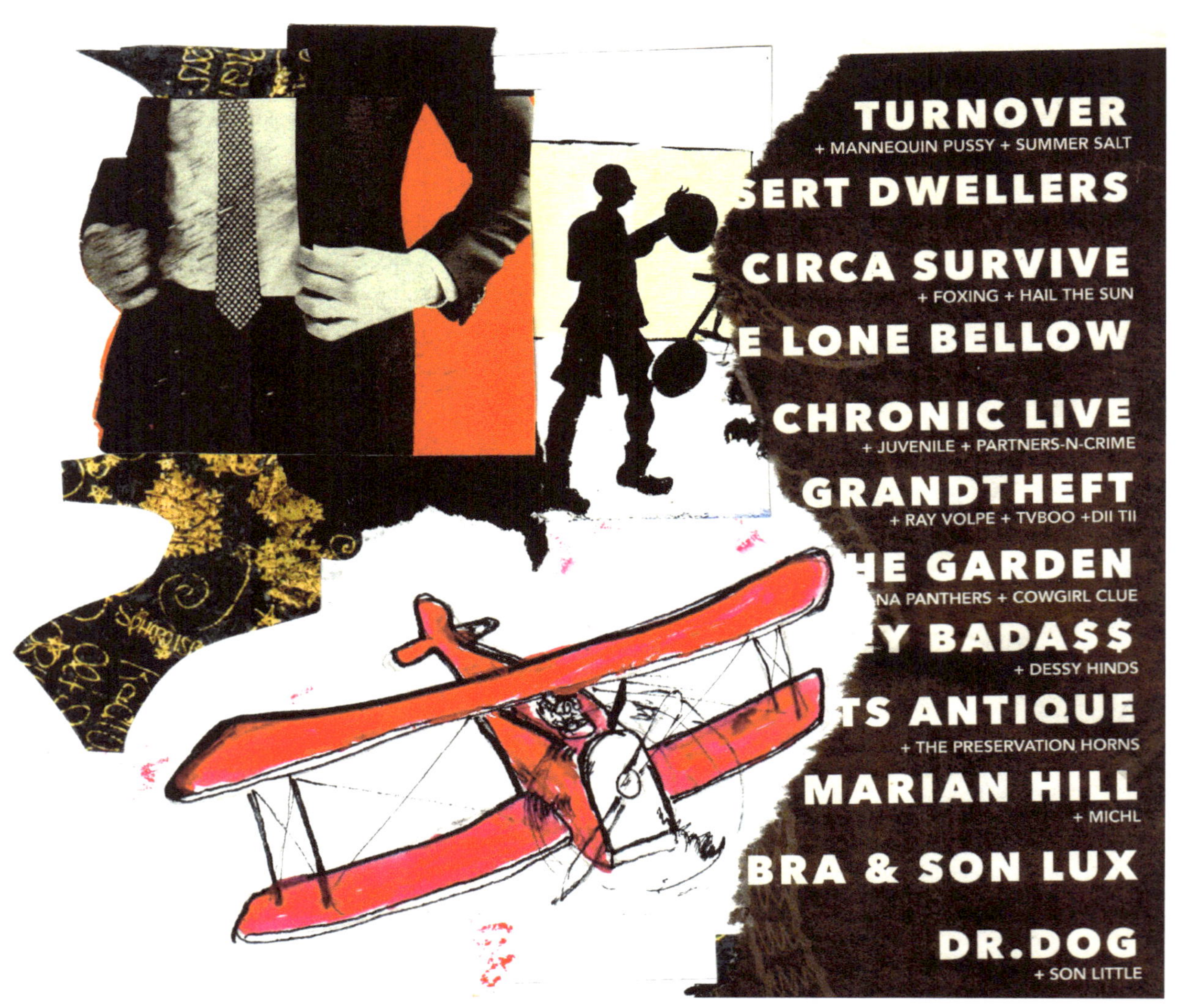

Jeffrey Cyphers Wright, *Badass* 2021 collage and ink on paper

JIM & ED

used to sit in this bar and sip margaritas for hours
and talk and talk until the cows came home, talk
in a way we don't talk anymore, talk a tad
courtly and courteous, even if they
weren't. I used to marvel what they did
with their retirement—interesting word, "retirement"—
to withdraw into seclusion—goes back
all the way to the 1500s. Before that, I guess they just
died on the job. Yes, I used to wonder what they did
with their time—and now I'm doing it too—killing time
in a pleasant haze as the booze settles in, the waitress
walks over with salsa and chips and says
she doesn't know where the time goes
while she's on her feet all afternoon,
The waitress is focused on serving,
not thinking about death. That's not
her job. That's my job. Her job
is to bring the drinks and chips
until we die. My job is to remind us
there are only so many drinks and chips.
What a waste, we say, and wag our heads, but time
takes us down a peg or two, whether we're making
it in Manhattan or on a rattan couch with some cat-woman
or volunteering time at the local cat shelter or bringing the spoon
up to the dim one's lips who's forgotten what a mouth
is for, and then, time takes us down
a peg or two more, and we might as well drink up
and order another margarita while we're at it, and some god-damn
hot salsa and salt-lime chips, if you don't mind me
getting specific and misty on you, saying what's really
on my mind, while we order what's left to order.

Gena Gruz*

VISION ON THE SUBWAY

1.)
The pressure gauge reads thirteen kilopascals.
The metronome tik-toks in the subway station.
Eleven apostles at the table. One more in the doorway.
Roman soldiers appraise the bacchanalia of a novel faith.
Who is pointing his finger at this Jew?
A best friend in sheep's clothing.

2.)
A pearl choker flirts with a fat wallet.
Dead souls in a dense breathlessness.
Despairing phones are suffocating life.
Girls play by the rules to strangle the person next to them.

IN THE DESERT

1.)
dromedary thoughts
the rider goes nuts
steps on the slimy sand
the desert has delirium tremens
the caravan keeps moving
a yellow yawn
the sun
the yellow eye of Egypt
has slept with eternity

2.)
"What load are you carrying?" asked the Immortal.
"My burden is to carry the cosmos on a hump and give you water
 so that you no longer live forever."

CONSTRUCTION SITE

beneath a red plastic helmet
a head protrudes from dirty overalls
a wrinkled neck above overalls
passionate cursing in deaf eyes
a pointy nose askew
a strong stale-cigarette smell
the crane is asleep
between the skyscraper and the shack

* Translated from Russian by Aaron Poochigian.

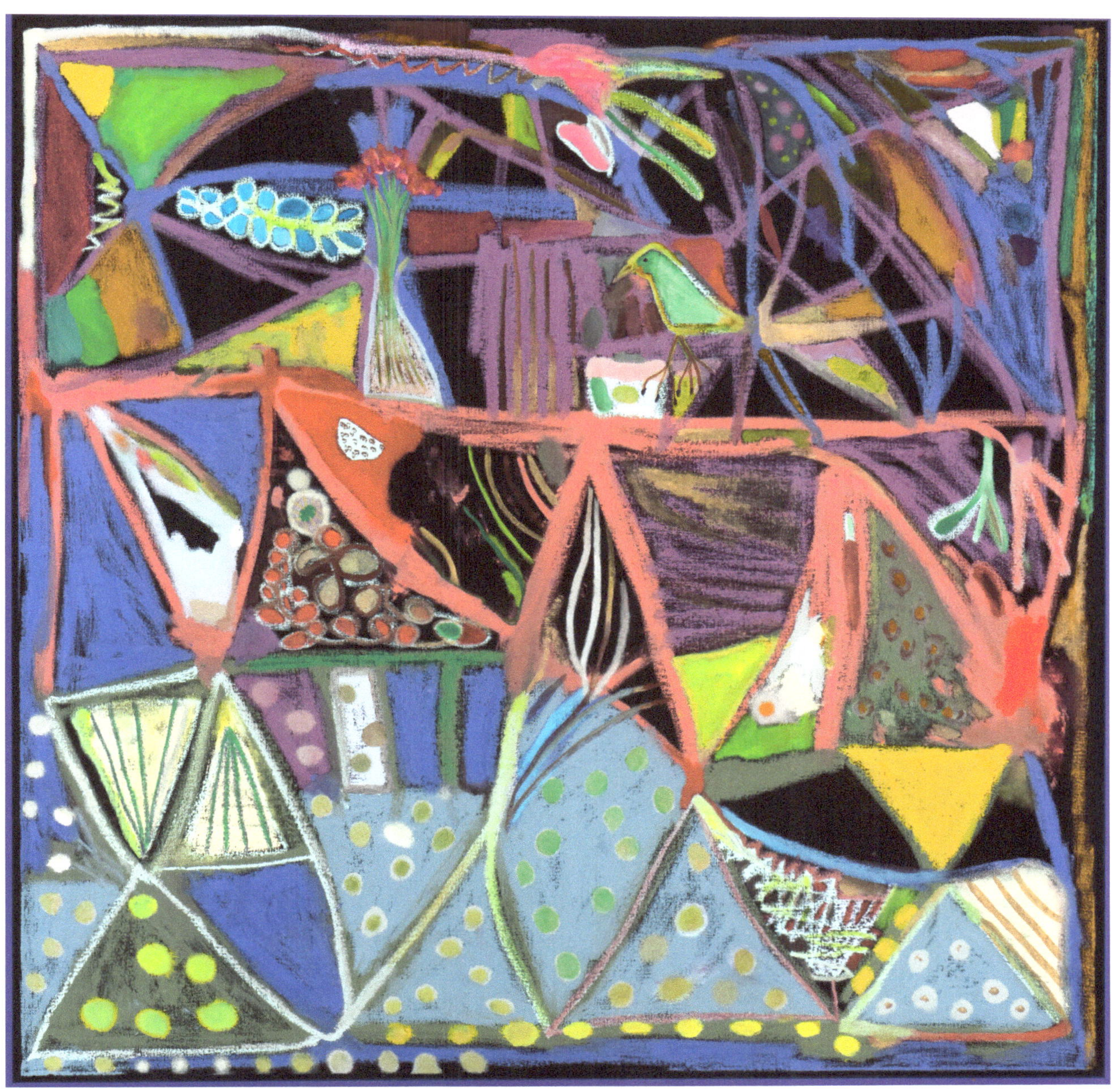

The Bird Nest Courtesy Nicola Vassell Gallery

Michael Lally

Question Everything

so says the poster
in this midtown Manhattan venue
and it has every
and thing
separated
as if they were two different words
which makes it seem like
things are to be questioned
as in the famous quote by
William Carlos Williams:
"No idea but in things"
which would mean going around
questioning tables and tools and
lamps and forks and, well, any
object, but it could mean
the way "thing"
has been used as a substitute for
penis,
which makes me imagine going
around with a microphone asking
penises questions
either literally, like actual dicks
or figuratively, like people who are penises
you know, dicks
but who wants to question
all the dicks in this world?
to what end?
there was a time when I wanted to, and did
question the dicks of the world
either in political debates or
radio interviews (I was what the old
use of the term "d.j." once meant back when
I was 18 in 1960 in upstate New York
and then in the early 'seventies
when I was in my early thirties and was a d.j.
on the first gay radio show, at least in DC)
or rhetorically questioned some of the dicks
in politics or the powers behind the politicians

in speeches I gave when
I was asked to talk at rallies and
protests and demonstrations and
man, I just remembered I used to quote
Karl Marx and say his favorite motto was
"Doubt everything" with the everything one word
in the translation I read
but he might have meant it as two separate words
and been thinking of dicks too.
Marx's favorite motto: question every dick.
I like it.

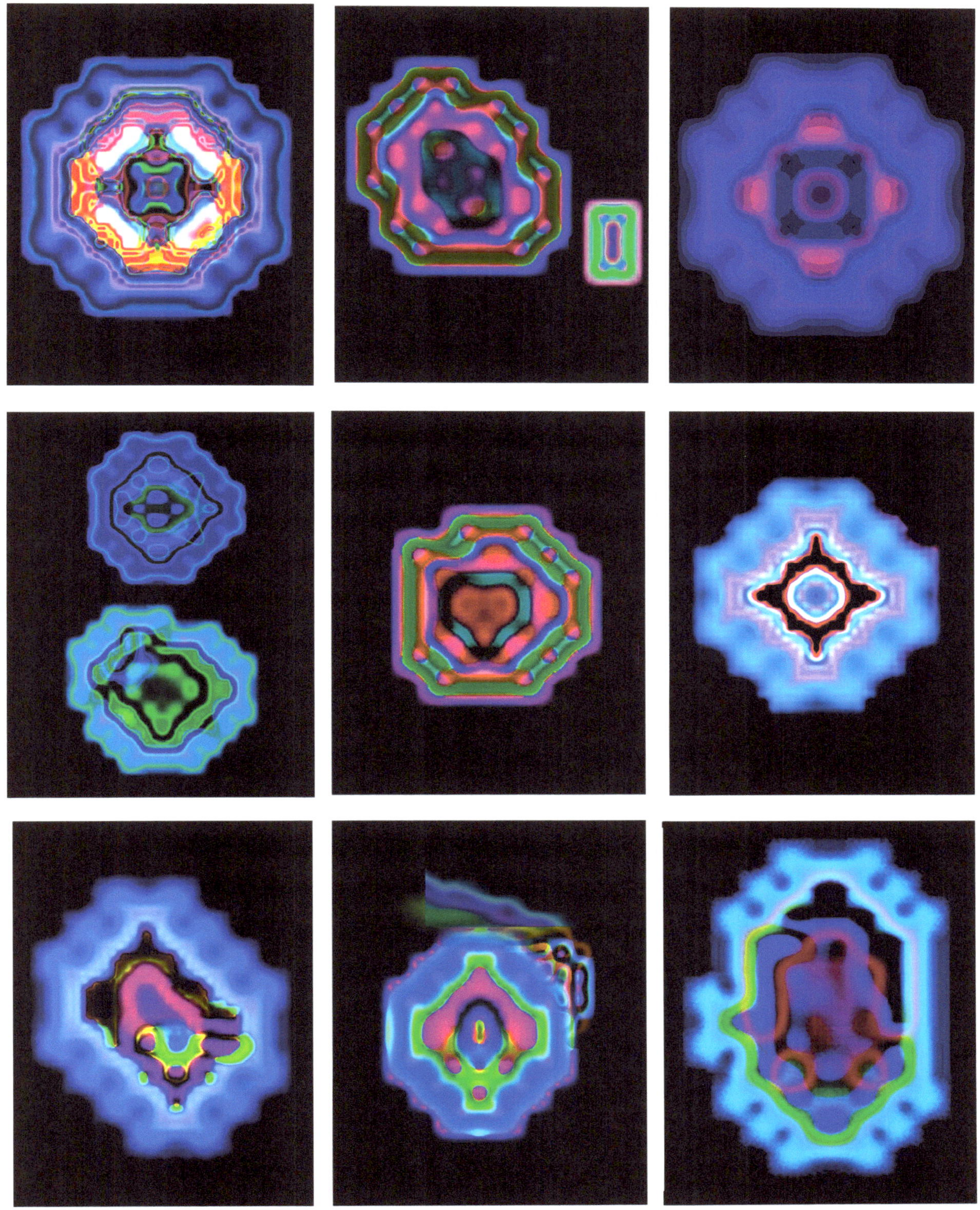

Mollies are available as NFT with additional video object.

Reviews

by Jeffrey Cyphers Wright

MINNESOTA DRIFT

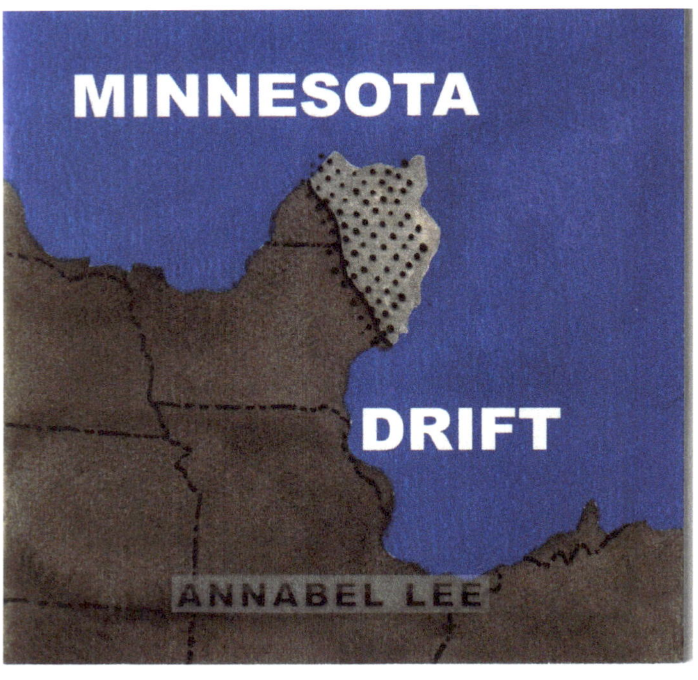

Minnesota Drift
by Annabel Lee
WryAwry 2021

Digging *Minnesota Drift*. Annabel Lee extricates a whole new animus in these chopped silk, frothy "emergency" "bleachers." Exquisite still-lifes done windmill style. Including (blush) "snatch power." With cover by Donna Dennis! (A Minnesotan). "basket moon   dream knocks." You'll be answering big time.

ON DIGIGRAM

Digigram
by Barbara Henning
United Artists Books 2021

DIG! These seemingly simple reflections, observations, thoughts, and memories are woven together in a way that creates surprises and epiphanies.

Barbara Henning has been developing her unique style of prose poems for her whole career, in a voice that is convincing, clear, and consummate. She touches all the touchstones from politics to age, ancestry, and sex. "you stuck your tongue in my mouth."

This poet's tongue will get stuck in your brain. Welcome *Digigram*, from the late Lewis Warsh's United Artists Books, (whose similar diaristic notebook style is equally seamless and consuming). Like strings of haiku, like beads of light.

WINGED RABBITS

The Winged Rabbits of Redemption
by Dave Roskos
Cat in the Sun Books 2021

Magic is wrung from the dust in Dave Roskos' razz-flown, beat up, cracked hallalujah Skeltonics.

In stripped down epistles of lyric loss and love, these poems nail down some shadow pain and outlaw glory. Searing portraits of the strugglers. Out of luck junkies, spacey inmates, and hapless hustlers. Mystic connections to a way-troubled dad. Dave is a resident Saint of the Underground. He puts patches on the soul.

IN NATURE, NOTHING EXISTS ALONE

(from *Silent Spring*, by Rachel Carson, 1962)

Curated by Laziza Rakhimova and Chris Costan
NYC Culture Club

This show of a baker's dozen, endeavored to wed aesthetics and environmental awareness and was largely successful. The artwork was by turns informative, spooky, prescient, and handsome.

In an accompanying statement, Chris Costan wrote that all the works "demonstrate the urgent need to live more responsibly given the Earth's finite resources." All of the art was informed by the urgency that is part of our collective zeitgeist in facing the existential threat of multiple ecological disasters and possible extinction of our species.

... artists confronting aspects of our planetary degradation in visually arresting ways.

The approaches varied from the vivid, Mordançage-altered photos of Laziza Rakhimova to painted and sewn pages by Elena Berriolo. Some artists used nature itself as a paintbrush. Oskar Landi created a machine to extract microscopic plastic filaments from Arctic waters. He then photographed the isolated material on the heads of pins and enlarged the images. The pervasiveness of our pollution is made manifest—and the implications are dire. Betsy Kenyon used the tides off Governor's Island to make marks on mylar in a cliché verre type of semi-photographic printmaking.

Also using the elements in a similar manner to Kenyon's marked surfaces, Kim Abeles used smog as pigment. She began experimenting with the *Smog Collectors* in 1987. She places stencils on top of blank plates which are situated on roof tops in various cities. Days or months later she removes the stencil and the images appear in the deposited smog. Apparently, World Trade Center execs vetoed images of Putin and Trump. The exhibition space directors replaced them with blanks.

At first blush, Valerie Hegarty's wall sculpture appears to be made of wood but it's actually epoxy clay and other materials. Roots protrude and branches twine together but join in an unnatural (rectangle) configuration. It's like an empty frame—a portrait of invisible irony—the vacuum humans are blithely accumulating.

It's encouraging to see these artists confronting aspects of our planetary degradation in innovative, thought-provoking, and visually arresting ways. Artists addressing our increasingly alarming situation are worthy of expanded and continuing attention. This is the best show regarding our very survival that I've seen.

The exhibition will be expanded for a redux at the United Nations later in 2022

—JCW, March, 2022

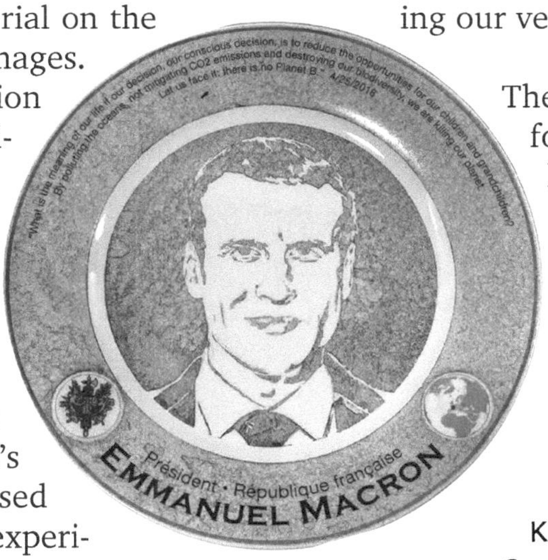

Kim Abeles
Smog Collectors

End Run

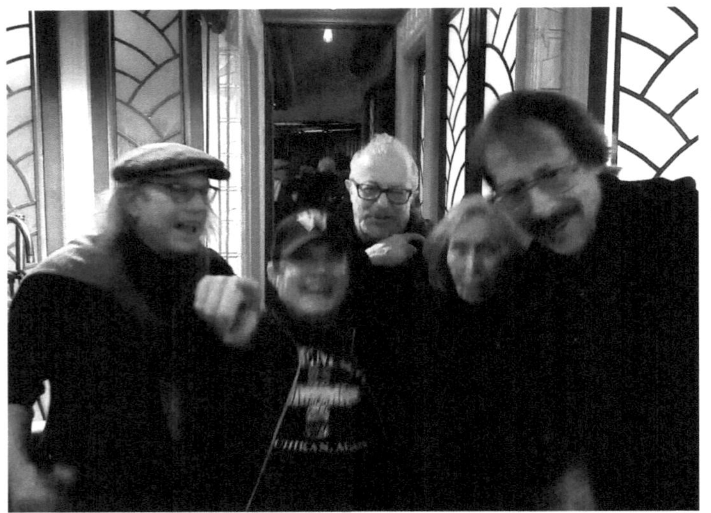

Poets at KGB, l-r: Steve Lutrell, Jeff, Andrei Codrescu, Yuko Otomo, Ron Kolm.

Dire urgency beseeches our attention at every turn, calling for focus and purpose. Let us go forth now in the service of deliverance.

KEEPING SPIRITS BRIGHT DEPARTMENT

For magnificent contributions to the arts, *Live Mag!*'s annual Lifetime Achievement Award goes to **Andrei Codrescu**. Encourager, energizer, endearingly "Exquisite." Andrei has published more books than you can dream of! Previous winners include **Bob Hershon, Willie Birch, Michael Lally**, and **Jane Friedman**.

HOTBED OF ACTIVISIONISM

Director Jane Friedman and *Howl! Happening* keep the lights on! The grand opening of a second space on the Bowery—Howl! Arts/ Howl Archives (HA/HA) conicided with an inagural show called "Icons, Iconolclasts and Outsiders" feauturing art by **Marguerite Van Cook, Brian De Palma, Scooter La Forge, Walter Stedding, Richard Hambleton**, photography by **Marcia Resnick** and **Gail Thacker,** and **Ramones** memorobilia designed by Howl's inspiration, **Arturo Vega**. All the work was from Jane's own collection and included several vitrines with seminal books by **Patti Smith, John Giorno, Richard Hell, Candy Darling, Allen Ginsberg** et plus.

THE FUN DOCTRINE

As an artist-in-residence at Howl! I participated in their *& friends* series, inviting friends to perform in "The Fun Doctrine." Four episodes are available on *Howl TV*. Performance with **Helixx Armageddon**; poetry and prose, **John Reed, Jose Castañera**, (DJ Uptown GI Jose), **Mike DeCapite, Ama Birch**; film, **Rita Barros, Luigi Cazzaniga, Lili White**; music, **Roger Manning**; art by **Kathe Burkhart, Chris Lee**; and puppets!

DOUBLE WHAM AT LA MAMA

La Mama hosted two *Live Mag!* events in 2021. It's always a major kick to work with **William Electric Black**. "Bustout Nation" featured **Patricia Spears Jones, Jose Padua, CA Conrad, Penny Arcade,** and artist **Carl Hazlewood** of *June Kelly Gallery*.

We came zip-roaring back for the "Nice n' Naughty" live show at the newly renovated theater on East Fourth. Special featured reader **David Henderson** was joined by a rollicking crew including **Adeena Karasick, Jerome Sala, Maria Damon, Sam Truitt**, with art by **Tamara Gonzales** and **Daniel Rosenbaum**. Thanks to the Poetry Electric Series. Working together for 15 years!

TOMPKINS ROMPIN'

NY Public Library Tompkins Square Branch mounted "Indy Indeed: A Half Century of Downtown Indie Publishing" curated by **Greg Masters, Ilka Scobie, Ron Kolm** and myself. The overiew included publications and ephemera from small presses including **Annabel Lee**'s **Vehicle Editions** and **Bararba Rosenthal**'s **Xanadu Press** with books by **Barry Wallenstein** and **Bonny Finberg**. Also **Hard Press, The Operating System**, *Mag City, Cover Mag, Vanitas, clwn wr, Tribes*, and *Live Mag!* Receptions with **Sheila Maldonado, Esther K Smith, Linda Kleinbub, Phillip Giambri**, and **Sharon Mesmer** accompanied the exhibit. Big thanks to librarian **Alyona Glushchenkova**.

SHOUT OUT DEPARTMENT

Yay **Rob Curcio**, curator of "The Rose Show" at *Mizuma and Kips Gallery* which included artists **Gregrory de la Haba** and **Claire McConaughy**,

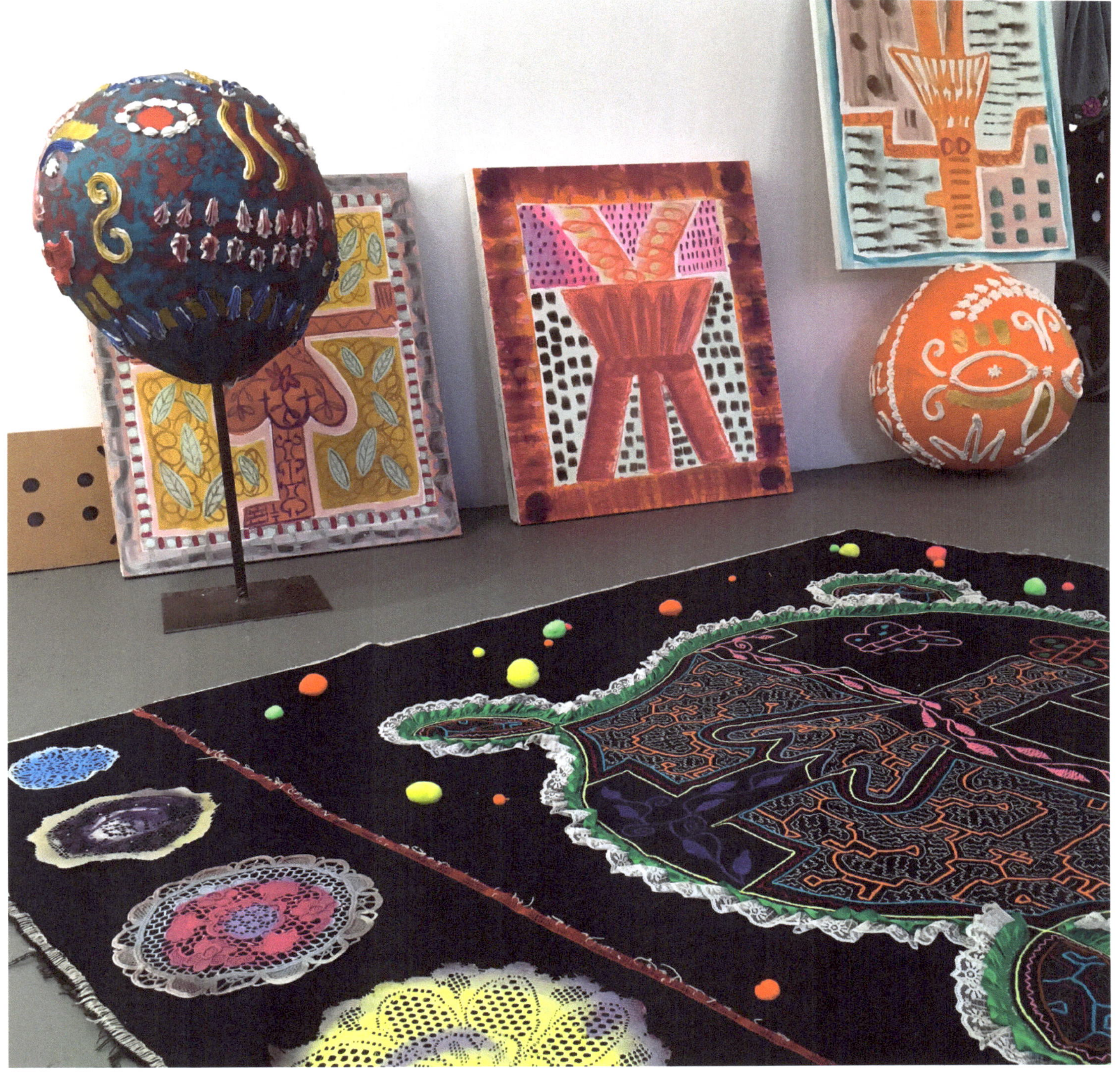

Tamara Gonazles, studio view

for hosting *Live Mag!* readers **James Feast, John Trause, Jan Castro, Gena Gruz,** and **Anton Yakovlev**.

Stepping out, **Arden Wohl** curated "Towering Minds"—the poetry series was a who's who of cool—**Kyle Dacuyan, Sparrow, Amy Lawless, Eileen Myles, Anne Waldman, Bob Holman, Mary Reily, Ilka Scobie** and me and more at *Tibet House.*

Jim Ruggia—Backroom Broadsides series.

Marc Vincenz and **Jonathan Penton** with their Saturday zoom *Lit Balm* series of readings. *Local Knowledge Magazine* and **Sanjay Agnihotri**. And big congrats to **Nicola Vassell** for opening a gallery on 10th Avenue and letting us share the work of **Uman!**

Finally, online: Check out the new artist and poet finder feature that **Lori Ortiz** designed! Enjoy the Edgy Issue! And Subscribe!!!

www.livemag.org

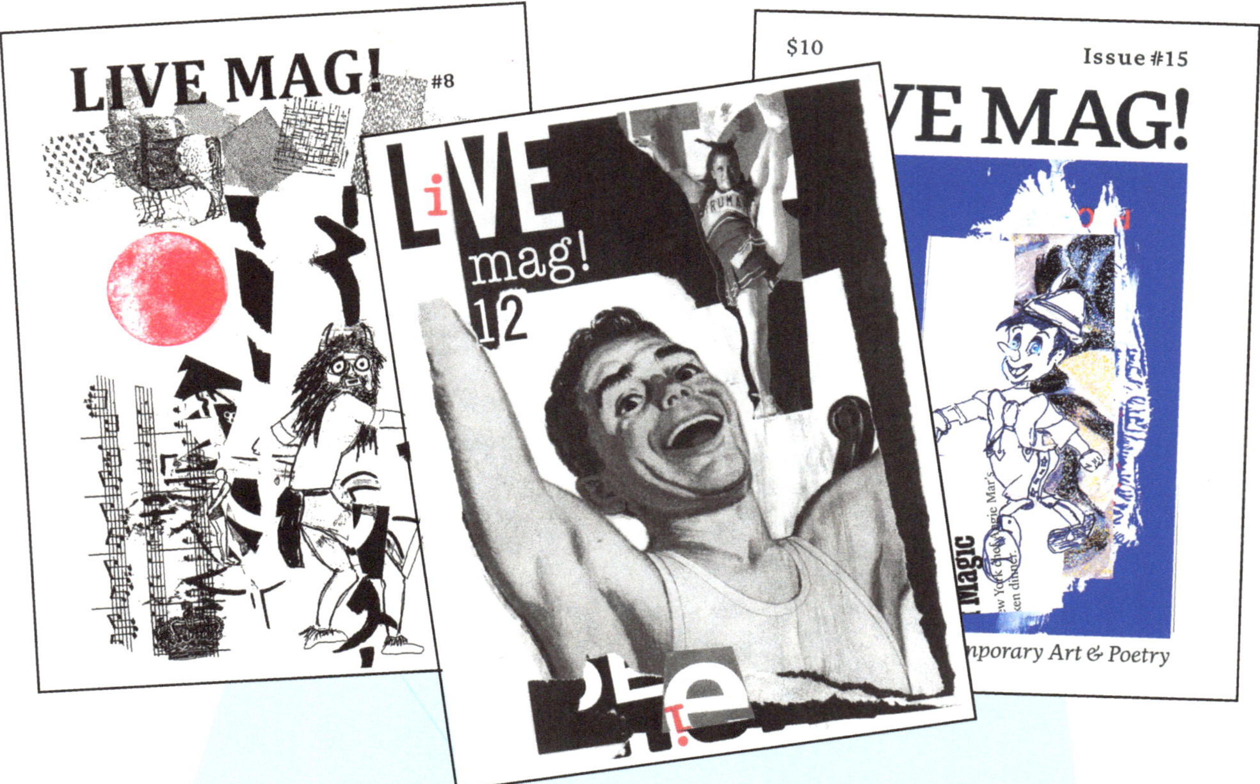

LiVE MAG!

From the stage to the page, from the wall to
the journal—each exciting issue is filled with
contemporary art and poetry. Snazzy, snappy,
and savvy—order a copy of Live Mag! TODAY!

Small editions and rare back issues with hand-embellished covers .
Order directly from Live Mag!
Issue 18 is also available from Ingram/Spark.

https://store.livemag.org